HEALING HERITAGE:
Paul Nordoff Exploring the Tonal Language of Music

Department of Music Education
College of Music
Temple University

HEALING HERITAGE:
Paul Nordoff Exploring the Tonal Language of Music

Edited by Clive Robbins & Carol Robbins

Barcelona
PUBLISHERS
TEMPLE UNIVERSITY
COLLEGE OF MUSIC
MUSIC EDUCATION AND THERAPY
T.U. 012-00
PHILA., PA

First Edition

ISBN 1-891278-06-1

2 4 6 8 9 7 5 3 1

Distributed throughout the world by
BARCELONA PUBLISHERS
4 White Brook Road
Gilsum, NH 03448
Tel: 603-357-0236
Fax: 603-357-2073
SAN: 298-6299

Managing Project Editor: Janet Frick
Designer: Terry McQuillin
Music Compositor: David Sampson
Text Compositors: Terry McQuillin and Saija Autrand
Cover Designer: Frank McShane
Front Cover Photo: Clive Robbins
Back Cover Photo: Rosemarie de Jongh
Photo Paintings: David McShane

Printed in the United States of America

"At length, when the appropriate wave
of the unseen lapped upon the shore of possibility. . . ."

Idries Shah:

"The Time, the Place and the People," in
Tales of the Dervishes

This book honors:

The Silver Clef Founders: Sam Alder, Dave Dee, Nancy Jarret, Andrew Miller, and Willie Robertson for riding that timely, benevolent wave. The enthusiasm with which you recognized the transforming potency of creative music therapy enabled it to become an ensouling, healing reality in the lives of countless human beings. Your generosity lives on in all who have been changed—and will continue to flourish in all who are yet to be changed—by the vibrant powers of the musical life you have supported and served so wholeheartedly for so many challenging years.

CONTENTS

EXPLORATION FIFTEEN
Pentatonic Harmonization and Styles of Improvisation

EXPLORATION SIXTEEN
Tonal Relationships That Link Archetypal Scale Forms

FOREWORD

During their years of pioneering work together, Paul Nordoff and Clive Robbins created an archive of clinical materials unlike any other in the field of music therapy. The archive contains written documents and audio recordings of their therapy sessions with clients, as well as lectures and workshops on their work for students and professionals. Spanning several decades, the archive provides a fund of knowledge of tremendous historical and pedagogical significance for generations of music therapists to come.

Healing Heritage is a carefully edited version of Paul Nordoff's "Talks on Music," a series of lectures given in 1974. I say carefully edited because Clive and Carol Robbins have been meticulous in preserving Paul Nordoff's voice, while also conveying his boundless passion for music and his unerring insights into its inner workings. But for me, this book is more than a monument to Paul Nordoff's enormous contributions to music therapy; it is a testament of the Robbins' dedication to their colleague, and a model of professional integrity for all of us to emulate. What tremendous respect these three have given to their work, and as a result to the entire field of music therapy.

Traveling through the sounds and words of the pages that follow is indeed a journey through music and music therapy, all under the guidance of a master composer, pianist, and therapist. Know that the journey through music is not idle musicological discourse, nor does it present fancy theoretical analyses that provide very little insight. These pages describe how each facet of music comes alive within us, and how music can bring alive our very being. And similarly, the journey through music therapy is not idle clinical discourse, with jargon saying nothing. These pages describe how therapy comes alive, and how it breathes new life into both client and therapist, all through the medium of music. Paul's dual perspective as musician and therapist opens up the worlds of music and therapy to completely new horizons.

Improvisational music therapy is not easily described in the few words available here, but when I read this book, I sense how when client and therapist improvise, they are building a vessel for themselves—a musical vessel that will take them through various realms of human experience, myriad forms of relationship, and many avenues within the therapeutic process. This vessel is where client and therapist will literally "live" their experiences together, not only as a safe therapeutic environment for self-exploration, but also as a place for adventure and risk, where both can dare to be with the other—freely, responsively, and communicatively. And in the end, this vessel will be the therapist's and client's gift to each other, for each will take leave not only with the sound memories of all the music they made together, but also with the new self discovered in the process.

Needless to say, it is important that the therapist have the ear, heart, and hand to create such musical vessels with clients. These vessels have to be safe, adventuresome, and beautiful places for both of them to share their musical lives. In this book Paul Nordoff, the master builder, tells how to build a musical vessel. Taking each element of music thoughtfully and lovingly, he shares with the students how to live in each tone, phrase, rhythm, melody, and harmony. This living the music is key, because it is only from within such experiences that a therapist can recognize the limitless potentials of music, and then utilize them with purpose and grace. To build the vessel is to live the music. This book is an exquisite guide to living music.

Kenneth E. Bruscia
Professor of Music Therapy
Temple University

ACKNOWLEDGMENTS

I would like to express my gratitude to the following people for their indispensable contributions:

Sybil Beresford Peirse, for the enthusiasm and dedication that made the 1974 Nordoff-Robbins Preliminary Training Course in Music Therapy a reality. Her total commitment to the furthering of this improvisational approach gained the support of leading managers and artists in the music industry, and so secured the practical and financial foundations on which it could continue to develop. From these foundations has come the funding which has underwritten the preparation of this book.

Carol Robbins, whose partnership with me made the planning and execution of the entire series of explorations possible. Without the keenness of her ear, her discerning musical perception, and her painstaking attention to every detail, the project could not have been undertaken. It is also an honor to salute her for validating, through the purity of her own creative work and her personal example of musical and clinical leadership, the therapeutic inspiration inherent in Paul Nordoff's teaching.

The students in the course, whose keen participation, integrity, and courage in undertaking a challenging venture into the unknown and unpredictable challenged Paul Nordoff to open to them a living world of musical spontaneity. Sissel Holten for her devotion, diligence, and utter dependability in recording the major part of the entire course. Jenny Bates for making the first selections, musical transcriptions, and summary texts of the original "Talks on Music." Jane Gibson (Jane Worthington during the course) for repeatedly testing the materials during the training course at the Nordoff-Robbins Music Therapy Centre, London, and for her helpful suggestions. Professor Alfred Neiman, himself a composer and teacher of improvisation to music therapy students, for his overall support and his contributions to the discussions. The many colleagues who have, at different times and in several countries, contributed in various ways to the project.

Joseph Fidelibus, Michele Ritholz, and Alan Turry of the Nordoff-Robbins Center for Music Therapy at New York University, for further help in transcribing musical examples; also, in this regard, Yuri Abe. A special appreciation must be voiced to David Marcus, who worked over the entire manuscript and made invaluable editorial suggestions. Kenneth Aigen, Jacqueline Birnbaum, Michele Ritholz, and Alan Turry for their editorial advice.

The officers of the Nordoff-Robbins Music Therapy Foundation, located in New York, who most willingly cooperated in funding the preparation of the manuscript: Ian Ralfini, President; Sunny Ralfini, Executive Director; and Melvin Epstein, C.P.A., Treasurer.

Kenneth Bruscia, Mary Lokey, and Bruce Saperston for the wisdom and guidance of their comments. The editing, design, and production team: Janet Frick, Terry McQuillin, David Sampson, Brigitte Pelner, and Saija Autrand, for sharing in a challenging project and for their diligence in shaping and completing the finished book.

Clive Robbins
Founding Director
Nordoff-Robbins Center for
    Music Therapy
New York University

INTRODUCTION

So all of music begins to look absolutely new through what therapy has made one realize about it. If it's become new for me, and can become new for you, and we can finish this course with the feeling that we have been on a great musical adventure—we have learned to use music in a new way, we have seen children respond and change—I think we'll all say we've had a very rich experience.

Paul Nordoff
Exploration Seven

A SHORT BIOGRAPHY OF PAUL NORDOFF

Paul Nordoff was born in Philadelphia in 1909 into a family that brought him a rich and varied musical life. He began his piano studies early, his vocation as a musician clearly evident. He studied at the Philadelphia Conservatory of Music, and with Olga Samaroff-Stokowski at the Juilliard Graduate School, New York. While at Juilliard, he relinquished his intended career of concert pianist and turned to composition, studying with Ruben Goldmark. As a composer, he received commissions for orchestral and vocal works, dance theater, and chamber groups; but throughout his career it was the writing of art songs that brought him special satisfaction. In setting poetry to music—setting *music to poetry* better describes his style of creation—he achieved an intimately natural unity of his love for poetic vision and his composer's imagination.

He received many honors for his work as a composer, among them two Guggenheim Fellowships and a Pulitzer Traveling Fellowship. He taught piano and composition at the Philadelphia Conservatory and Michigan State University, and from 1949 to 1958 was professor of Music at Bard College, New York. He was a brilliant pianist, with wide musical experience and tastes, and gifted with what was to become the foundation of his subsequent contribution to therapy in and through music—an extraordinary talent for improvisation.

In 1958, while on sabbatical in Europe, he encountered by chance the use of composed music for therapy with physically disabled children in Scotland, and the use of improvised music with speech-impaired children in Germany. Intrigued by the therapeutic possibilities of live music and the implications for composition and improvisation, he visited Sunfield Childrens Homes in Worcestershire, England, a residential school for developmentally and multiply disabled children and adults, with a long tradition of applying the arts as forms of developmental and educational therapy.

These experiences affected him profoundly and brought him the realization that it was more meaningful to devote his musicianship and creativity to exploring the therapeutic powers latent in music than to continue composing and teaching in the conventional sense. His life changed in every respect: musically, professionally, and personally; he abandoned his academic career and began investigating the literature and practices of the then newly developing discipline of music therapy.

His visit to Sunfield Childrens Homes formed an important connection: he admired the professional staff he met, and felt drawn to the warm, creative ambience he had experienced there. His proposal that he begin his experimental investigations at Sunfield was welcomed, and in September 1959 he joined a treatment research team headed by the research director, Herbert Geuter, M.D. Immediately Paul Nordoff began collaborating with staff members in composing songs and musical activities, and in exploring the application of improvisation as a versatile communicative medium for severely, profoundly, and multiply disabled children.

It was at Sunfield, where I was a special class teacher, that my collaboration with Paul Nordoff began. I joined him at this stage in the development of an original approach to music therapy. For some years I had felt profound frustration at the seeming impossibility of penetrating the communication barriers of profound developmental disability and autism in children. Paul Nordoff's application of improvisation and composition, and the expressive directness of his musical presence, were now demonstrating ways of reaching through these barriers; with some children his approach brought deep and significant changes. As we collaborated, conducting courses of therapy, investigating responses, and developing methods of documentation, child after child exemplified the width, depth, and potency of human susceptibility to a virtually limitless world of musical expression and form. We also began to compose songs and other musical activities with specific therapeutic intent. The children's personal and social gains confirmed the effectiveness of a creative approach to music therapy.

After the initial developmental period at Sunfield, and a European lecture tour, Paul Nordoff and I demonstrated our approach with children at the Department of Child Psychiatry, University of Pennsylvania; and at the Devereux Foundation, Pennsylvania. This led to a succession of music therapy treatment and research projects over the next seven years in different areas of pathology and in various clinical and educational settings. The two largest were concurrent: a five-year treatment, training, and research project with autistic children at the University of Pennsylvania, funded by the National Institute of Mental Health; and a demonstration, treatment, and training program with developmentally disabled children in the School District of Philadelphia. The work attracted support—other grants underwrote research studies and funded the writing of instructional texts.

From 1967 onward Paul Nordoff and I taught extensively and wrote, principally in Scandinavia, Germany, and the United Kingdom. This stage of our lives culminated in 1974, with an invitation from British colleagues to establish a treatment and training center in London—beginning with a concentrated six-month course entitled the "Nordoff-Robbins Preliminary Training Course in Music Therapy," at Goldie Leigh Hospital, London.

As his partner, I was aware that in our shorter courses prior to the London course, Paul Nordoff had begun the massive task of bringing together his two musical lives. He had integrated all he had vividly experienced over the fourteen years of music creatively realized as therapy for disabled children, with over thirty years of study, college teaching, composition, and performance that had preceded his work in therapy and laid the groundwork for it. I had the intuition that the Goldie Leigh course would be uniquely significant and made the decision to record it completely. It is from transcripts of recordings of his "Talks on Music," as they were originally entitled, that *Healing Heritage: Paul Nordoff Exploring the Tonal Language of Music* has been prepared. I could not know at the time that this course would represent in one sense the culmination of Paul Nordoff's life's work. Shortly afterward he became ill, and although he was able to contribute to a subsequent course in 1975–76, his condition deteriorated and he died in February 1977.

THE SETTING OF THE COURSE

The content, purpose, and thrust of Paul Nordoff's teachings are to be more fully understood in the context of the Goldie Leigh course, and in their bearing on the students' overall training and clinical work, so some background on the course itself will provide orientation.

The course was called the Nordoff-Robbins Preliminary Training Course in Music Therapy, and it focused on improvised musical experience and expression as the main attributes of an intercommunicative treatment modality for variously handicapped children. It had the dual intent of developing students' clinical competence while increasing their musical proficiency and resourcefulness. The training was consistently based on practical application. It was given at Goldie Leigh Hospital, a children's hospital in which the principal therapy room doubled as the lecture room, and this served to reinforce the clinical orientation of all instruction.

From the beginning of their training, the students observed individual music therapy sessions conducted by the instructors. As individual students became sufficiently prepared, they were paired into teams to undertake supervised clinical practice. In the team relationship, all gained experience in each of its roles—as primary therapist at the piano with one child, as cotherapist with another. Students with previous music therapy experience or greater musical confidence began their work with children first. By the eighteenth week of the course all students were in practical sessions. At this stage, with sixteen children in weekly individual sessions, an active and diversified field of musical and clinical experience was developing. The children presented a variety of contrasting conditions, individual needs, sensitivities, and modes of response.

The students' learning continuously evolved as they worked in their individual ways and circumstances at applying the musical resources, techniques, and clinical approach they were assimilating. All students observed each other's work from an observation booth and shared in subsequent discussions. For the purposes of documentation, guidance, and analysis, every session was audio-recorded in an open-reel stereo format; the session was recorded on one channel, and an accompanying clinical commentary made by Paul Nordoff and myself on the other.

Practical, theoretical, and musical instruction pertinent to clinical application was given throughout, both in direct relationship to the current work, and through clinical studies prepared from courses of therapy conducted previously by the instructors or by associated clinicians. Related subjects included piano and vocal improvisation, documentation, evaluation, child psychology, the management of courses of therapy, and the practical use of equipment—all subjects contributing to developing the practice of clinical musicianship.

The musical foundations of clinical musicianship in therapy concerned Paul Nordoff deeply. These lay not only in each student's clinical ability and musical skills, but in his or her *musical awareness,* in the experiential knowledge of music and the understanding-feeling for the expressive dynamics of its melodic, harmonic, and rhythmic components. He believed such a perceiving knowledge to be indispensable to the responsive, creative application of music in therapy. In his explorations of music, he sought to impart his experience as a composer and therapist to his students, and to arouse in them the intuitive insights that were intrinsic to his life of musical inspiration. He would not allow any traditional, accustomed, or biased thinking about music to blind a student to the creative possibilities a musical response to a situation might hold. No aspect of music could ever be passed over superficially, nor could tastes resulting from enculturation limit musical horizons.

His creatively free, experimental practice of music therapy had led Paul Nordoff into a profound reexamination of music, a refocusing of his own composer's perceptions. In the explorations in this book he shared his journey with his students; he wanted to bring to them a compositional awareness of musical elements, components, styles, and idioms that might enable them to impart more direction, order, and musically communicative intent to their uses of improvisation. Throughout the course, he worked to elevate his students to a level of musical spontaneity that transcended mere technique, however capable this technique may have become. It was his hope that his students could release in themselves, and so experience and develop, the creative sense of immediacy and expressive freedom that was so characteristic of his own clinical work.

The explorations were directly related to instruction in improvisation. In the coursework, an exploration often directly preceded or followed improvisational instruction in the same musical subject. Some explorations included improvisation instruction as Paul Nordoff called on students to help investigate and illustrate the subject. After the course, when recordings of his teaching were being compiled for use in subsequent training courses, he suggested that as much as possible the explorations be separated from the improvisational instruction, and presented as a course of study in themselves as they were also of generally wider interest. We have followed this procedure in preparing this text.

THE STUDENTS

The fifteen students who participated in the explorations formed an international group. Eleven were qualified pianists, three had previously combined piano with other studies, namely medicine, psychology, and special education. Four, including the tutor for the course, had completed the postgraduate diploma course in music therapy at the Guildhall School of Music and Drama, London. Three students had recently participated in a two-month introductory course we had given in Norway. Four had been practicing therapists for up to five years. They were:

Sybil Beresford Peirse, Tutor for the Course	United Kingdom
Jenny Bates	United Kingdom
Anna Viciani Bellini	Italy
Merete Birkebæk	Denmark
Annelise Dyhr	Denmark
Jean Eisler	United Kingdom
Jane Gibson	United Kingdom
Jane Healey	United Kingdom
Sissel Holten	Norway
Unni Johns	Norway
Nancy McMaster	Canada
Tom Naess	Norway
Knud Onstad	Norway
Elaine Streeter	United Kingdom
Amanda Warren	United Kingdom

Professor Alfred Neiman of the Guildhall School of Music and Drama, London, audited parts of the course and at times contributed to the discussions.

THE RELEVANCE OF THESE EXPLORATIONS TO OTHER CLIENT GROUPS

Throughout the development of Paul Nordoff's and my work, from 1959 through 1974, we had concentrated on music therapy with children. The approach and practice we pioneered became known as "Creative Music Therapy," after the title of our book by this name. The application of its principles, practice, and philosophy to adult clients was undertaken by colleagues and former students, initially in Scotland and in Germany, in the years immediately following this and the subsequent Goldie Leigh course.

The communicative powers of music used creatively proved to be effective in a variety of treatment settings, including geriatric and psychogeriatric care, adult psychiatry, medical treatment, and intensive care. Developments over the following thirty years broadened this responsively creative practice to include:

> All areas of special education
> Programs for developmentally disabled adults
> Psychiatric hospitals and clinics for all age groups
> Community mental health centers
> Programs for substance abuse disorders
> Rehabilitation programs for the physically disabled
> Treatment programs for HIV/AIDS patients
> Hospitals for the elderly and for patients needing extended care
> Palliative care
> Stress and anxiety reduction
> Alleviation of pain
> Counseling, including loss and bereavement
> Correctional institutions
> Private practice

PREPARING THE TEXT

In editing the transcripts of the original explorations, I have continually asked myself, How would Paul Nordoff have wanted them edited? What digressions would he have wanted to delete, what clarifications or supplementary information would he have wanted to include? In coming to editorial decisions I had constant recourse to our seventeen years of teamwork as music therapists, researchers, writers, and teachers. We had collaborated on four books, numerous studies, and countless presentations, and as we moved from project to project and country to country, we had maintained a continuous and widening dialogue about the work we were developing. This lived history of collaboration guided the approach and determined the procedures through which the manuscript was prepared. It was also important that my co-editor and wife, Carol Robbins, who began studying Paul Nordoff's work in 1966 and knew it extremely well, had not been among the students on the Goldie Leigh course and so could bring an appreciative but objective perception to editorial decisions.

There were editorial challenges inherent in the historical and practical circumstances in which this instruction was given and in how the recordings were made. The recordings were of a once-only event, there was no prepared script, there were no retakes. Paul Nordoff knew the musical dynamics of the compositional elements he wanted to explore and communicate to his students, and he had a sense—from supervising their clinical training and from their progress in his improvisation classes—of what their needs were, and how ready they were for what he wanted to give them. Inevitably, the dynamic of improvisation was present in how he led into his subjects and mediated the explorations. A further factor was that he was teaching in London; his own musical library was in Spring Valley, New York. Most of the musical examples he played were from his memory, which served him remarkably well considering that he had played very little of the repertoire he used for illustration since he had begun investigating music therapy fifteen years earlier. Many of his examples must have been summoned from still deeper levels of his memory.

ON THE TYPOGRAPHY

This book is an edited transcript of recordings of live, eventful teaching. Paul Nordoff's mode of communication to his students consisted of a freely expressive mixture of speech, piano playing, and singing; at times he also invited the students to speak, play, and sing, then wove his teaching around their participation.

Integrating this complex blending of words and music into a transcript that could attempt to capture the animated spirit of the original explorations, yet be capable of transmitting their content smoothly and intelligibly, presented specific textual challenges. In the many passages where speech and music are closely entwined—where music serves to demonstrate the spoken content, or speech serves to elucidate a musical reality—a particular typographical convention has been adopted to indicate the temporal relationship between what is being said and what is being played. I have adapted the use of series of periods, which normally indicate ellipses, to indicate that speech has momentarily ceased and that music is being played and/or sung. Three periods . . . indicate that music is playing. These may be followed by speech or descriptive editorial additions to the text, for clarification of actions such as [playing into the fifth measure] or [Jane repeats the example.], or to give supplementary information. These are given in brackets and italics. This device links music, speech, and "action" to denote that a train of thought, or line of exploration is being followed. The addition of a fourth period . . . . indicates music being played to an ending, or necessary punctuation in the text. [Occasionally, where an entire sentence is enclosed in brackets, the first of the four periods falls within the brackets and the other three follow outside, like this.] . . .

In preparing the book, two other requirements had to be fulfilled: the printed text had to represent what was originally spoken as completely as possible in spirit and in content; and all musical examples, exercises, diagrams, and technical illustrations that were demonstrated aurally to the course participants—and/or written on the blackboard—had to be available to the reader. Throughout the text, the relevant musical notations and figures are interleaved with the text as they occur in the explorations. Specific references to melodic, harmonic, or rhythmic components are identified by numbers in parentheses, i.e. (12), in both the musical score and the text, so that the reader can easily refer back and forth.

Paul Nordoff made frequent use of notation or diagrams on the blackboard, either referring to materials previously written out, or writing them out as a subject was developed in class. All essential scores and diagrams are reproduced. There were many times when he referred to a tone, harmony, phrase, or other specific musical component by indicating it on the blackboard; we have endeavored to minimize confusion in these situations by identifying each subject by name or by numbered reference in the text.

THE RECORDINGS

The compact disc recordings of this course are not issued with the text.
Inquiries regarding their availability should be directed to:

Nordoff-Robbins Center for Music Therapy
New York University
82 Washington Square East
New York, NY 10003
U.S.A.
phone (212) 998-5151   fax (212) 995-4045

Nordoff-Robbins Music Therapy Centre
2 Lissenden Gardens
London NW5 1PP
U.K.
phone (171) 267-4496   fax (171) 267-4369

A CONCLUDING PERSPECTIVE

Paul Nordoff's creative initiatives in music therapy and in his teaching sprang from the integrity of his personal and professional musical life, and not less from who he was, spiritually and artistically, as a searching individual of his time. Inevitably, his contributions reflect the temporal placing of his life span within the context of the ongoing evolution of music, and are oriented toward the sociophilosophical attitudes toward treatment and healing that were developing at the time and that fashioned the environment in which his work was done. In no sense is his teaching to be taken as a "last word" on the subjects with which he was so intensely concerned, but as a deeply considered and musically practical introduction to a vast—but little explored—world of human experience and potentiality. His teaching does not preclude further elucidation, but invites it. His pioneering explorations indicate directions for deepening research and raise questions that subsequent generations of music therapists may be moved to answer. I hope that clinicians practicing in later, contemporary styles will be inspired to extend the explorations, and so to disclose the Healing Heritage inherent in the music in which they sense their identity.

Clive Robbins

HEALING HERITAGE:
Paul Nordoff Exploring the Tonal Language of Music

EXPLORATION ONE
SCALES: STEPS AND SKIPS

*R*eexamining the scale as part of a rediscovery of music. Hearing the scale as a musical experience, and as a distinct musical statement. Becoming sensitive to melodic and harmonic dynamics in the relationships between tones in the scale. The importance of scale passages in melodic construction; balancing the compositional use of stepwise tones with skips of melodic intervals. Examples of the sensitive, inspired, judicious balance of steps and skips in melodies of Beethoven, Bach, Mozart, Ravel, Schumann, and Gershwin.

THE DYNAMIC PROPERTIES OF SCALES

[The students first consider scales. When asked what are their associations with scales, they offer a diversity of responses: practicing; excitement; creating moods; dreams; concentration; challenges; "something to be gotten through"; distaste; ambivalence; the spiraling character of scales; learning the relationships among keys; one scale growing out of another; the connections among scales, key signatures, and the circle of fifths; and the satisfaction of technical accomplishment.]

What is a scale? I'm thinking of major scales, minor scales, and the modal scales—what is a scale?

There are seven tones, played successively; they have relationships to each other, and the scale ends with the fundamental tone an octave higher. Is that a satisfactory definition? If anyone can think of a better one, please let's have it.

Jenny: Could you repeat it, Paul, please?

Paul: I don't know if I could, Jenny: Seven successive tones, which end on the ground tone, or the first tone, an octave higher, and these tones have a relationship, one to each other, and one to all of the rest—each to each other and each to all. Is that true? What else can we say about the scale as a musical experience?

Elaine: Certain tones are more important than other tones in terms of the harmony.

Paul: Certain tones in the scale have become more important than others, because on those important tones we have based a system that revolves around them, that gives the scale or the composition what we call its tonality. Those important tones, the first tone and the fifth tone—the tonic and the dominant, and the fourth tone, the subdominant—give us the tonal center of the harmonies of the scale. But I am really not yet that far, I'm still talking about just the scale itself. What is it as musical experience?

Jane H.:   Each scale has its own individual character, which is independent of its pitch.

Paul: If we take all the majors, all the minors, etc., all the modal scales on the twelve different notes, one after the other—and we say we find each one different—all the major scales are similarly constructed, so why should they be different? One is higher than another, and one has different overtones than another. As a composer, I think Alfred *[Professor Neiman]* would agree with me that every scale is absolutely different in its possibilities for composition.

Alfred: Absolutely.

Paul: And that you can't possibly begin a composition until you have the right key for it.

Alfred: Absolutely right.

Paul: You just cannot imagine this:

EXAMPLE 1-1. Beethoven, *Piano Sonata in C Major*, op. 53, "Waldstein," opening.

. . . *[plays the first three measures in C major, then in F major]*. . . . You can't imagine it in F major! It's just inconceivable!

SCALE PASSAGES AND SKIPS IN MELODIC CONSTRUCTION

Now, let's go on. What more can we say about a scale? What is done with it? What does it present?

Elaine: You rearrange it melodically.

Paul: Melodically! Thank you, Elaine.

In the construction of melodies—and we're talking about after the fact, we're not talking about actually manufacturing them, we're talking about looking at the inspired melodies of composers—we find the enormous importance of the scale in melodic construction. You find this beautiful, sensitive, controlled, inspired balance in melodies of composers. We find, when we look at the melodies of the music we love—of Mozart, of Beethoven, Schumann, Debussy, whomever—we find this wonderful sensitivity in using notes in sequence that come from the scale in which the composition is written, with skips of melodic intervals.

I am telling you this because it is part of our reexamination of music. It is part of our rediscovery of what lives in music that we can hope to absorb and use in our work with children, particularly melodically in the songs we write for them, the songs of greeting and the songs of goodbye.

There's the scale, D major:

[plays the scale with emphasis on each note]. . . . That's a statement. First of all, you must think of the scale as a statement *[repeats the scale]* . . . and what it is stating is its presence, its potentiality, its creative self.

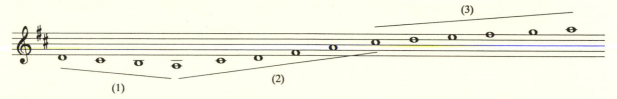

So, when one of our very best composers does this first (1) and then does this (2) and afterward (3), he has done something wonderful to the scale. And the scale has said to itself "Thank God!" So what do we have?

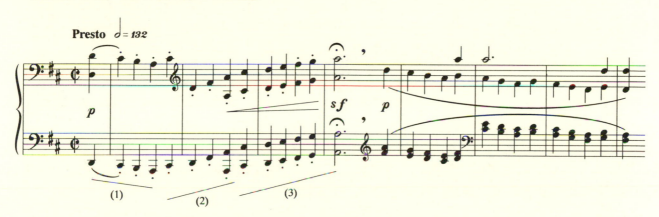

EXAMPLE 1-2. Beethoven, *Piano Sonata in D Major*, op. 10, no. 3, opening.

. . . we take the first tones down . . . we go down to the dominant (1). At the end we ascend to the dominant (3) . . . and in between . . . the tonic triad appears (2) in the middle—those are the skips—and . . . the C♯, which leads us again into the ascension of the scale back to the dominant (3). . . . So what has he done? He has first taken us to here (1) *[reviewing the tonal directions on the blackboard]*, and then he takes us to here (3), and the whole piece just pours out of these notes.

Alfred: May I emphasize what you've said, Paul, with the fact that that little arpeggio, of course, dramatizes that scale wonderfully, and those leaps *[more accurately, "skips"]*—

Paul: —the leaps follow the leading tone to the tonic *[playing (2)]* . . . the one, three, five of the tonic triad, skipping again to the leading tone, and then up. We have this wonderful balance of the scale passage beginning, the leaps in the middle that just touch on the tonic chord—because this is in a fast tempo—but the melody indicates it, settles the tonality, and ends again with the scale passage. So there you have a beautiful balance with the skips in the middle and the scale passages on both sides.

Well, now let's look at some more:

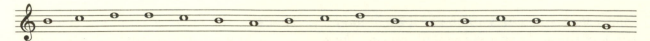

There aren't many leaps there, are there? *[playing the melodic line as written]*. . . . You would say that's a pretty dull melody, wouldn't you? But when it goes:

EXAMPLE 1-3. J.S. Bach, *Chorale* from *Cantata 147*, "Jesu, Joy of Man's Desiring" (transcription by Myra Hess).

. . . and so on. This is something I think we can really get down on our knees to. Not only what the man has done with this chorale melody, and many of these chorale tunes are just as simple as this—most of them are. But not only that he has done it, but that we can listen to it. We can look at it; we can see that this beautiful embroidery that rises and falls also consists constantly of steps and skips and steps and skips! *[playing the transcription and singing the melodic elaboration to emphasize its steps and skips]*. . . . It's scale up and down, scale up and down. It's just fantastic what happens!

Look at your music! Look at these wonderful, wonderful things. And when you practice your scale exercises, think of them in a different way!

THE SCALE AS A MUSICAL STATEMENT

Knud, will you play this for us at the piano please *[writing scales on the blackboard]:*

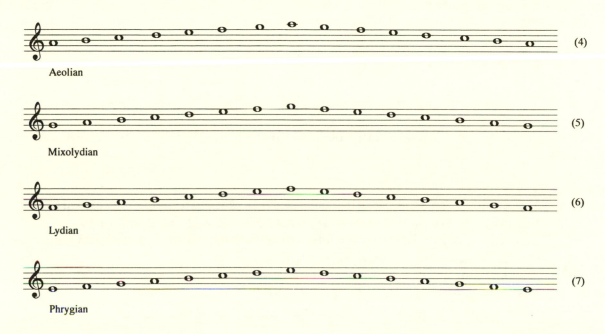

[Knud plays each scale in turn. . . . He repeats them as the students name them.] . . .
What is the name of this one (4)?

Students: Aeolian minor. . . .
Paul: Aren't you lovely smart people! And this one (5)?
Students: Mixolydian. . . .
Paul: Mixolydian! Oh, so beautiful! And this one (6)?
Students: Lydian. . . .
Paul: Oh, you're all getting so smart I don't know what to do. And this one (7)?
Students: Phrygian. . . .
Paul: Phrygian, almost my favorite. All right, thank you, Knud. May I get to
           the piano?
Clive: You know what it's going to be?
Paul: Do you? Do you know what it's going to be?

continued on next page

continued from preceding page

EXAMPLE 1-4a. Mozart, *Piano Sonata in C Major*, K. 545, measures five to nine.

. . . . Now, how often have you heard this played *[repeats the section fast and superficially]* . . . ? Pretty often!

Jenny: Yes. I hate it like that!

Paul: Many people do. But in each measure there is a statement, and Mozart has made it. He hasn't written in these scale passages for fun, or for decoration. And what do they come after? What kind of a melody? What has gone on in the melody preceding this?

Amanda: It's very simple; it starts on the tonic.

Paul: Yes *[begins playing, focusing on the melody].* . . .

EXAMPLE 1-4b. Mozart, *Piano Sonata in C Major*, K. 545, first four measures.

But they're skips, aren't they? *[measures one and two]* . . . with a turn at the end. Skip again *[measures three and four]* . . . and a step to finish. What is supporting this? The same thing *[plays the first two measures with the left hand accompaniment].* . . . And the thing is so full of joy and light! Usually you look at it and you think this is so simple. Oh, God! the poor piano student thinks—

Clive: Music box music.

Paul: —try to learn to play these scales.

DYNAMICS OF SCALAR MOVEMENT

[Plays the ascending Aeolian scale (4) on A, as in the Mozart sonata]. . . . All right! So you begin a scale *[plays A]*, from the fundamental tone the experience is going to come *[repeats the scale]* . . . you move through the subdominant and you move through the dominant, but you do more than that. *[playing to illustrate]* You move . . . through this *[B]*, which wants to

go back *[A]* . . . and you are taking it forward *[B on to C]* . . . all right, it will go forward! *[D]*. . . . But the C has its harmonic relationship to A and *[playing the tones of the A minor triad]* . . . to E, and C also its melodic relationships to the B that precedes it and the D that succeeds it. You go on to the D and the same thing happens . . . it is the same with every tone of the scale. There is a force in each one of these tones. There is dynamite in each one *[plays the Aeolian minor scale]*. . . . And to play it with this kind of joy, of recognition!

When Beethoven begins the piano part of the *C Minor Piano Concerto:*

EXAMPLE 1-5. Beethoven, *Piano Concerto in C Minor*, op. 37, solo piano entrance.

. . . with these ascending scale passages, three of them, sparks absolutely fly! *[speaking-singing the first three measures of the piano entrance . . . and the tonic triad (8)]*. . . . The tonic triad!—which we've all heard five thousand times! But it's the way it's done, it's the context in which we hear it. It's the fact that this scale in its place, at that moment, says "Here I am!"

STEPWISE MOVEMENT IN THE BASS

But this wonderful balance that you find in all of this music! May I show you something in D-flat?

. . . [*slowly playing Db up to Gb and back to Db*]. . . . It's going to do this in the left hand in the bass. Then it's going to do this [*C–Bb*] . . . two more steps. Then it's going to skip, a big daring skip, to a fourth [*F*] . . . and then back to the tone it hadn't hit before [*Ab*]. . . . This is the bass of:

EXAMPLE 1-6. Ravel, *Menuet* from *Sonatine.*

. . . [*playing into the fifth measure*] . . . and so on. This beautiful dignified minuet of Ravel from the *Sonatine.*

And, Cherubini, I think it was, who said, in answer to some question, or in the right context, about who was a great composer—how can you tell a great composer? "By their basses ye shall know them!" And that's a beautiful remark. Look at Beethoven's basses, look how they move:

EXAMPLE 1-7. Beethoven, *Piano Sonata in E Major,* op. 109, third movement.

. . . the beautiful rising stepwise, scalewise rising of the bass in that slow movement!

Ravel had a particular sensitivity to this beautiful balancing of stepwise passages and of skips in the construction of his melodies. One sees this in the very simple, but fantastically beautiful first piece in the *Mother Goose Suite, Ma Mère l'Oye*. It's called the *Pavanne of the Sleeping Beauty,* I think. Now this is one of the simplest possible things anyone has ever written, certainly in our time. There are two melodies, one in each hand:

EXAMPLE 1-8a. Ravel, *Pavanne of the Sleeping Beauty,* first four measures.

. . . the lower voice moves up . . . these five tones (9). The upper voice . . . moves up stepwise, then in downward skips (10) with an upward step in between, and they meet on the dominant . . . just as clear as a sheet. . . .

Alfred: Very classical.
Paul: Absolutely marvelous! *[continuing playing].* . . . Then what comes next:

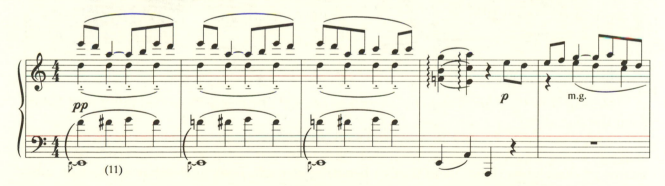

EXAMPLE 1-8b. Ravel, *Pavanne of the Sleeping Beauty,* measures five through nine.

. . . (11) a real feeling of fairy tale. . . . Look at the music you are studying! Notice how the composer has used scalewise progressions, and how he has balanced these with skips. Then when you use a goodbye song—and I liked Sybil's "Goodbye, Robert"—

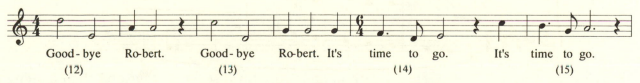

EXAMPLE 1-9. Beresford Peirse, *Goodbye, Robert.*

with its skips of a seventh: "Goodbye, Robert" (12). . . . "Goodbye, Robert" (13). . . . What did she do then? "It's time to go" (14) . . . no more big skips, "It's time to go" (15). . . . Perhaps we could have even fewer skips than there are there—as a contrast. Perhaps—it's just a question in my mind.

It is perfectly possible to have a marvelous melody with no steps in it at all, just as it's possible to have a melody with no skips in it at all. And when we practice our improvisation this week, the right hand has got to begin now, and the left hand, to find its way into melodic construction, over the intervals the other hand will be playing. This is the kind of food that nourishes this ability. I assure you of that.

When I speak of a composition with big skips, you can hardly beat this one:

EXAMPLE 1-10. Schumann, *Davidsbündler*, op. 6, no. 12.

[Playing the first four measures]. . . . Schumann! Tiny little scale passage and then leaping all over the keyboard! Absolute freedom! Simply marvelous; then what happens? *[plays*

measures five through eight]. . . . Quite contained. Then *[measures nine and ten]* . . . off he goes again. Glorious composition! One page long and worth its weight in—what! It's from the *Davidsbündler;* it doesn't have a name, I don't think, that particular one. But the whole *Davidsbündler* of Schumann is a mine of musical treasure for the music therapist to refind how intervals are used, how melodies are constructed, how harmonies move and change—all the things we'll be dealing with, working with, more and more as time goes by.

And it's very interesting that you find this sensitivity among the really gifted popular composers as well. Gershwin had it, for instance:

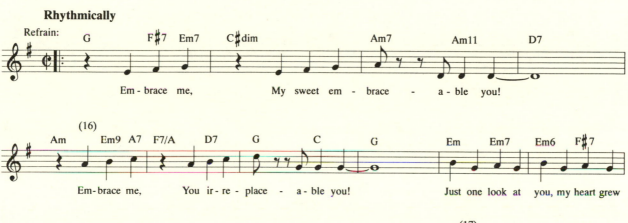

EXAMPLE 1-11. Gershwin, *Embraceable You,* refrain.

. . . *[playing and singing into the fourth measure]* . . . there's the skip. We start a little higher (16) *[continuing into the eighth measure].* . . . It goes on and finally *[singing into the twelfth measure, then playing and singing measures thirteen to sixteen].* . . . *[The students laugh with surprise and pleasure.]* That glorious octave descending leap (17) after those ascending scale passages!

Alfred: It's easy to listen to, jolly hard to write.
Paul: It certainly is hard to write. It's a great piece; it's going to live forever!
Alfred: Great skill.
Paul: Absolutely!

So look at the greeting songs and goodbye songs that you will be improvising and composing. And when you work on your improvisation exercises, you can have as a general principle the thought that you can alternate and balance stepwise passages with skips—skips along the lines of a chord or not. There's no reason why they should be *[plays C, E♭, G]* . . . skips along a tonic or dominant triad. We want more freedom than that. But what we would like to have would be a sensitive musical balance between these two elements.

All right, let's stop, shall we? *[begins playing a song for closure]:*

EXAMPLE 1-12. Nordoff and Robbins, *Goodbye!* From P. Nordoff and C. Robbins,
The First Book of Children's Play-Songs (Bryn Mawr, Pa.: Theodore Presser Co., 1962), p. 21. Used with permission.

[The session closes as the students join in the song.]

EXPLORATION TWO
STEPS, SKIPS, AND CREATIVE LEAPS

Exploring the inherent tonal directions of scale steps within one octave in the Phrygian mode. An experimental examination of the melodic potential inherent in the movements of tones and the relationships between them. The force and activity within tonal movement; the satisfying natural directions of melodic movement intrinsic to every tone. Stepwise movement and certain melodic skips as inherently natural directions of a tone. Making a creative leap by taking a tone beyond its natural directions. The need for such creative leaps. Evolving tonal relationships into sequences. Revitalizing the dominant-tonic relationship. Bringing an awareness of the meaningful dynamic reality of each tone into the therapist's fingers and voice, thus intensifying and increasing the livingness of improvisation.

EXPLORING INHERENT TONAL DIRECTIONS

Jean, will you help me today in a new exploration of the single tone in its relation to other tones in the scale? Doesn't that sound beautiful! The single tone in its relation to other tones in the scale.

You've got to have a tone to begin a piece of music. Or perhaps two—sometimes two are enough.

From the tonic upward

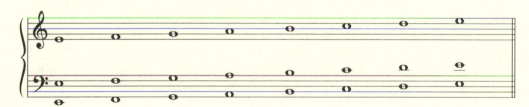

Let us use the Phrygian mode on E. Play E with the right hand, and play the octave in the left hand with it: E. . . .[1] Pause, hold the tones. That's a challenge, isn't it! Really listen to it. Play it again: E . . . something is going to happen—what? Who is going to have the enormous courage required to leave the safety of this harbor? *[Throughout the exploration each tone played on the piano is tripled in the lower middle register of the keyboard, with a single tone in the right hand and octave in the left.]*

Play it again: E . . . how secure it is! How comfortable one can feel in a single tone! How one can identify with it! How lovely that nothing has happened but this one tone, in which we can live and imagine almost anything. But we're going to do a very daring thing; we're going to play it: E . . . then we're going to play F: F. . . . *[All the following explorations of tonal directions are played slowly and deliberately; the tones are held.]*

That's a daring thing! We have left the safety of our harbor; we have opened up the possibilities that lie in E by just taking it to its next tone in this beautiful scale.

---

[1] The typographical convention "E . . ." signifies that E is held while played or sung; "E . . . F . . ." signifies that first E, then F are played or sung, each tone being held. A fourth period "E. . . ." indicates the end of a sentence and/or melodic phrase.

From the second scale tone

What does the movement E to F contain within it? Play the two tones again: E . . . F. . . . It contains a force, it contains an activity, it contains a direction—are you with me? In which direction does this tone wish to go?

Students: On to G. Back to E.
Paul: How many think it wants primarily to go back to E? *[four students]* Everyone else thinks what—that it should go up to G, it wants to go to G, its direction is pointing toward G? Don't be creative, listen only to this tone.
Elaine: Actually, I don't want it to go to G; I want it to go to F♯.
Paul: Yes, but you can't have F♯, my dear; you're living within the limitations of the Phrygian mode. You can't have everything you want in music any more than you can have everything you want in life. Play it once more, E . . . F. . . . Can we all just sing it, without the piano: E . . . F. . . .
Clive: It wants to stop there.
Jean: I want it to stay there, yes!
Paul: It's so beautiful you want it to stay there, but if we're going to have music it cannot stay there. So that we have that possibility, that the tone wants to stay. Or we *think* it wants to stay.
Jean: It was probably the crescendo in the voices.[2]
Paul: There is the possibility that the direction of the tone leads back to E. Why? Because it is so close to it, it's the next neighbor to it.

There is also the possibility of the direction to G. So let's have them both: E . . . F . . . E. . . . Very satisfactory, we're back safe in our harbor, we haven't risked a thing. We haven't lost a cent. We've had a nice experience without paying for it. Are you still with me?

Inherent Ascending Directions								
	F	*G*						
Scale tones	E	F	G	A	B	C	D	E'
Inherent Descending Directions		*E*						

FIGURE 2-1. Here and throughout, the prime mark (as in E') indicates a note in the octave above the original one.

Now let's take the other direction that lives in this tone: E . . . F . . . G. . . . Ah! Now we still have music. We still have more possibilities, because where does the new tone want to go? We have answered a question with a question, which is what happens in music all the time. *[retracing the steps on the diagram]* So we have done this, we have found out we have this possibility *[E–F–E]*, and this possibility *[E–F–G]*, and also the possibility in a limited sense, the possibility of stopping there. And now having taken this direction, we have asked another

---

[2] Also, at this early stage in the exploration, the sense of the Phrygian tonality with E as its tonic is not yet established, and E moving to F may be implying the leading tone moving to the tonic in the key of F.

question. Will you play the three again, Jean? E . . . F . . . G. . . . You can almost feel a pull to get that F to G, because it is a whole step, and not the F♯ that Elaine mentioned.

Sissel:	I want it to go up to B.
Paul:	From where? From F, can we hear that? *[E–F–B]*: E . . . F . . . B. . . .
Sissel:	It's from Grieg! *[Piano Concerto in A Minor, op. 16, first movement. Everyone laughs with recognition and surprise.]*
Paul:	That's right! That's an association. A composer has done it! A composer has had that beautiful imagination to use the tritone melodically. How it lives in you—it's part of you forever! Wonderful thing!

From the third scale tone

Now, let's play E–G without the F: E . . . G. . . . What are the directions in G? Where is this tone reaching out? What is it reaching out to experience?

Jane H.:	Because E has come before, I feel it's going to B.
Paul:	You feel the B, all right. Let's play E . . . G . . . B . . . *[sings to complete the opening phrase of the first theme from the first movement of* Piano Concerto No. 3 in C Minor, *op. 37, Beethoven. Students join in singing the phrase; again there is laughter.]* It's in the wrong key!

There again, a composer has done it! Isn't it wonderful to make these discoveries! But your hearing the G go to B could be conditioning. Because then you have completed the minor triad, which is part of our whole harmonic system and which you have been absorbing, digesting, hearing, playing, for many years in your life.

So, let's go back to E–G: E . . . G . . . and try to wipe out all associations. Let's sing it again: E . . . G. . . . This G really wants to go somewhere, doesn't it, not just to that B. A— yes indeed, that's a possibility.

Jane H.:	F.
Paul:	F is another possibility.
Sissel:	Up to the E'.
Paul:	Up to the E'? Let's listen to that: E . . . G . . . E'. . . .

Immediately we're getting into the realm of creativity. We're taking the G outside of its direction; we're skipping the entire rest of the scale in order to do it. We've made a creative leap, and out of these creative leaps, melodies—and therapy—are born. So that's a very good one, Sissel, but the inherent directions are as we are finding them.

Inherent Ascending Directions	*F G*	*G*	*A*					
Scale tones	E	F	G	A	B	C	D	E'
Inherent Descending Directions		*E*	*F*					

FIGURE 2-2.

Can we hear E . . . G . . . F . . . ? That's nice. That should give you a real feeling of satisfaction. Something quite inevitable has taken place, something logical and true! In these movements of tones, in their relationship in the scale, lies something we can actually call truth. You can demonstrate it, because this is it.

Let's sing it without the piano—don't slide: E . . . G . . . F. . . . Wonderful experience!

Including the fourth scale tone

Now let's play E–G–A again: E . . . G . . . A. . . . We are really making progress now. We have arrived at a new tonal experience; a new tone with a new direction, a tone that asks a very penetrating question indeed.

Inherent Ascending Directions	*F G A*	*G*	*A*	*B*				
Scale tones	E	F	G	A	B	C	D	E'
Inherent Descending Directions		*E*	*F*	*G F E*				

FIGURE 2-3.

Can we play E–A, please? E . . . A. . . . Again: E . . . A. . . . Now don't suddenly say you feel you're in A minor, because you're not! We're not playing *sol–do*! We're playing *do*, E, and from E we've done *[sings stepwise up to]* A . . . we've arrived here. What are the directions?

Knud:	Up to B.
Paul:	Up to B is obviously one of them.
Nancy:	Can you have the direction that it should be repeated? Is that a direction?
Paul:	That is a possibility, but not a direction. Does that answer your question?
Nancy:	Yes, it does!
Jenny:	I'd like to go back to E.
Paul:	You'd like to go back to E. So that is one possibility. I'll put the point of the arrow on E. Anyone else feel another direction in this A?
Jane H.:	Back to G.
Paul:	Certainly. You see this tone has more directions in it; it has more places to go.
Amanda:	What about F?
Paul:	You think F is there as a direction?
Amanda:	Sure!
Paul:	So do I, very strongly. So now, we want to listen to E–A–F: E . . . A . . . F. . . . That's wonderful too, isn't it! And E–A–G: E . . . A . . . G . . . so is that. You know, there's something alive now that wasn't living before! And now E–A–B: E . . . A . . . B . . . that's a marvelous one, isn't it!
Unni:	Grieg again! *[Death of Aase from* Peer Gynt Suite, *no. 1]*
Paul:	Grieg again. I tell you, they were canny men, those composers!

All right. So we have found—let's just count the directions we already have in four tones. *[counting]* We have already eight directions possible for four tones in their relationships.

Now all of this is therapeutic material, but it must live in your fingers with the dynamics that belong to it. Not just as notes to be played, not just as something that lies under your hand, but each tone in its meaningful dynamic reality.

So now let us sing E–G–F: E . . . G . . . F. . . . Good, now let's sing E–A–G: E . . . A . . . G. . . . We have something quite wonderful already, we have a kind of sequence there, just made of tonal relationships. *[sings the phrase]* Very beautiful. You can add rhythms to that *[sings]:*

. . . . You've got three completely different experiences because of the different rhythms with which you have endowed these tones.

Including the fifth and higher tones

Now we're going to do this: play E–A–B: E . . . A . . . B. . . . It's very interesting that when you play E–A–B, you don't feel such a strong dominant-tonic relationship between the B and the E. Play the E–G–B: E . . . G . . . B. . . . Now you feel the direction of B is *[sings E]* to go back to that tonic. But if you play E–A–B: E . . . A . . . B . . . it frees you from the triad, doesn't it? And you feel more the possible directions contained in the tone B.

Jean:	It could go up to C.
Paul:	Certainly, it's pulling toward the next tone in the scale, definitely; particularly if you know the Phrygian mode, and you know there is just a semitone now to the next tone higher. Play it again, E–B will be enough: E . . . B. . . . Where else can it go? Where else does it want to go?
Jane W.:	G.
Paul:	Yes, certainly, G lives in it.
Unni:	E.
Paul:	The top E?
Amanda:	The top E'.
Unni:	The bottom E.
Paul:	The bottom E?—back again to the starting place. Is that what you meant?
Amanda:	Yes, but when some of the students said the top one, I realized it also wants to go back to the first one.
Paul:	All right, it wants to go both ways.
Knud:	To the D as well *[sings E–B–D]*, I heard that.
Paul:	Can we play E–B: E . . . B . . . now let's play D: D. . . . What do you think? Is that a direction in the tone or is that a creative leap?
Students:	A creative leap.
Paul:	It's a creative leap.
Jean:	Not at all, I felt that D might come from the fourth, from the A *[plays E–A–D].*

Clive: It immediately wants to go on to something else.

Knud: *[sings E–A–B–D]* That was it.

Paul: You mean after the E–A–B? Play E–A–B: E . . . A . . . B . . . now the D:
            D. . . . But it's very interesting: if you would play E–G–A–B–D:
            E . . . G . . . A . . . B . . . D. . . . That's very satisfactory, isn't it? If you've
            had pentatonic experience, that is a very satisfactory progression. It is
            actually in a mode of the pentatonic scale and not in the more familiar
            form of the scale, which here would begin on G and end on E. But most of
            us feel that B–D is a creative leap.

Can we have E–B again? E . . . B . . . we can do C . . . or we can do—stay on the B: B . . . *[sings]*
B . . . G . . . E . . . E'. . . . Is there anything else that lives in here? Don't you feel that B also,
as a direction toward the note from which it's come? Most of them do.

Inherent Ascending Directions	*F G A B*	*G*	*A*	*B*	*C E'*			
Scale tones	E	F	G	A	B	C	D	E'
Inherent Descending Directions		*E*	*F*	*G F E*	*A G E'*			

FIGURE 2-4.

INHERENT DIRECTIONS AND CREATIVE LEAPS

Can we sing E–B–A: E . . . B . . . A. . . . That's really lovely. Let us add it: *[The students sing
as tones are pointed out:]* E . . . F . . . E' . . . E' . . . G . . . F . . . E . . . A . . . G . . . E . . . B . . .
A. . . . They are all beautiful, and how each one seems to intensify! There seems to be more
force, somehow, in this one *[E–B–A]* than in this one *[E–A–G]*, because of this big interval to
which we have gone before we have returned, and this *[E–A–G]* is in between the two. But
the dynamic quality—the livingness—seems to increase.

So now we've got five directions in the B—and so it will go, you see. Now let's take
E–B–C, and then repeat the C: E' . . . B . . . C . . . C. . . . Wonderful! When you get to that
sixth, I tell you we're sailing out of our harbor! We're well on our way.

Let's consider the directions in C. Who hears what? *[Students give suggestions.]* So you
hear the return to B; someone heard the D; Clive heard the top E'; A, I hear, very strongly.
Anything else?

Let's hear it, shall we? E–C–B: E . . . C . . . B. . . . That's a nice movement out and then
to a resting place; and the next, E–C–D: E . . . C . . . D. . . . We're still sailing; the wind is
blowing us.

And E . . . C . . . top E'; E'. . . . What do you think of that? Does that really seem to live
in the C as a direction? Or do you feel that as a creative leap?

Students: Creative leap.

Paul: Isn't it strange, one does feel it as a leap; it doesn't seem really to be one
            of the directions of the C. So let's take this one out.

Clive:	It almost comes to a stop, doesn't it.
Paul:	Yes.
Elaine:	That's because it implies the relationship of C.
Amanda:	Can you play it once more? *[Jean plays]:* E . . . C . . . E'. . . .
Paul:	It can't stop there, in any case, can it?
Amanda:	But I think the connection between the E's is too strong to say it's a creative leap.
Clive:	It's coming to a kind of rest, isn't it?

COMPLETING MELODIC PHRASES

Suppose you play the E–C–E' again, and then take it back to B: E . . . C . . . E' . . . B . . . . That feels good, doesn't it! Feels very good. Why? Because we have gone back to one of the directions that really lives in C, interposing a tone in between. And this happens in music all the time.

Inherent Ascending Directions	F G A B C	G	A	B	C E'	D		
Scale tones	E	F	G	A	B	C	D	E'
Inherent Descending Directions		E	F E	G F E	A G E	B A G		

FIGURE 2-5.

Can we have the E–B–C, and back to A: E . . . B . . . C . . . A . . . . How do you feel about that? Shall we sing it? E . . . B . . . C . . . A . . . feels like a direction of C to me.

Knud:	It completed the phrase for me.
Paul:	Now it's a completed phrase we're singing, of course. *[sings, extending the phrase]:*

You can go on with this phrase and develop it, and vary it, and repeat it, and intensify it. We have created a phrase.

   And now—very interesting—we have agreed that C has one fewer direction than the dominant, it's interesting, one fewer than the B. It feels absolutely inherent and natural to it. Now let's take the E–D: E . . . D . . . beautiful, isn't it? Play it again: E . . . D . . . . Marvelous. Yes?

Jane H.:	B.
Paul:	B, all right. Let's hear that: E . . . D . . . B . . . how does that seem to you?
Unni:	Complete.

Paul: Again, we have really interposed a tone between E and D, haven't we, by taking it to B. And this is creative. At the same time, I think that the direction to B does lie in D. Who hears something else in D?

Students: Top E'.

Paul: The top E', of course! Play it again: E . . . D . . . E'. . . . Yes, that's wonderful! Let's sing that: E . . . D . . . E'. . . . That's a marvelous experience! That really is a great experience.

Jean: C.

Paul: Right you are, Jean. Play it: E . . . D . . . C. . . . And that again is a further intensification of the phrase we've had before.

Jenny: I found that rather a flattening experience.

Paul: From D—

Jenny: D back to C.

Paul: E–D–C?

Jenny: I find it less satisfying than E–D–B. I don't know quite why. It's an anticlimax somehow, that C.

Paul: Let's hear it again: E . . . D . . . C. . . .

Jean: It wants to go on to B.

Paul: Yes, that asks a question—*[Jean plays B]*—or anywhere where the C would go. *[Jean explores, plays]* D–G and D–A.

I think we're back again to three directions. We've gone from two directions, to four, to five, to four, to three. It's very interesting.

Inherent Ascending Directions	*F G A B C D*	*G*	*A*	*B C*	*C E'*	*D*	*E'*	
Scale tones	E	F	G	A	B	C	D	E'
Inherent Descending Directions		*E*	*F E*	*G F E*	*A G E*	*B A G*	*C B*	

FIGURE 2-6.

Now let's start on different tones of the scale and use their directions. Let's start on the G and use the two directions we felt in it. G . . . A . . . F . . . E. . . . Can we sing? And play and hold the E on the piano, just the E: E . . . and we'll sing: G . . . A . . . F. . . . Isn't it lovely! *[The students express their enjoyment.]* You don't have to sing the tonic—one can still hear it; it's living *behind* the tones we sing.

   Let's take, on the C, the same two directions *[Jean plays]*: C . . . D . . . B. . . . E. . . . Let us sing the notes there *[with the E on the piano still sounding]*: C . . . D . . . B. . . . Keep the E sounding! Now from the G: G . . . A . . . F. . . . *[Students express satisfaction.]*

   These are beautiful tonal experiences. This gives one some idea of what lives in a scale as dynamic musical force!

   With the C, we also had the A. We can put it anywhere, so let's add the A to our chart. Play the E . . . and we'll sing: C . . . D . . . B . . . A. . . . Now let's sing C–A–B–D. Play the E again: E . . . *[class sings]* C . . . A . . . B . . . D. . . . The room is absolutely full of music! All kinds of things are happening—possibilities of what can be done with these wonderful tones. Let's take the directions of another tone.

Tom: When you stop at that point, a child must sing with you! *[Students laugh.]*
Paul: He really, nearly should, shouldn't he! Maybe some would!

ENLIVENING THE MELODIC ROLE OF THE DOMINANT

All right, let's play the bottom E, and we will sing the directions of B: B . . . C . . . A . . . E' . . . C . . . G . . . A. . . . This is just *play* with the various tones that live in B as directions.

So the dominant is not a dead duck yet! It becomes dead only when it's used in a dead way. It becomes dead only when it becomes something you have no control over. It becomes dead only when it's overused. It becomes dead only when its other directions are not explored, and when all you can think of is *[sings]* B–E. Let's sing it: B . . . E . . . that's not the end of the dominant, is it? That's not the end of B at all! *[sings:]*

. . . quite a different thing! So explore what lives in that tone, and take your time before you introduce this relationship, which has become so corny—unfortunately—the direction back to the tonic.

THE NEED FOR CREATIVE LEAPS

Now, it is quite possible to do something exciting in a different way. If we observed only those directions that live in each tone, in the way we worked, we would be enormously restricted. We must have creative leaps. But the moment we make a creative leap—and I'm going to make one now—the moment we make a creative leap, then we must work with what lives in the tone to which we have leapt.

So we know, from this little silly chart *[indicating Figure 2-6]* that if we leap to a tone, we have the choice of moving to tones that belong to its natural directions. So, if Jean will play the E again, and we'll sing E–A and then follow me, all right *[pointing out tones from Figure 2-6]*: E . . . A . . . B . . . F . . . G . . . A . . . E. . . . *[B–F and A–E are creative leaps.]* Have you ever done anything prettier for a child? And it's all there *[sings]*:

. . . . Beautiful melody!

Let's take another creative leap: to the C. *[Jean plays E]*: E . . . all right, we'll sing E–C, and then we'll play with these *[pointing out the tones]*: E . . . C . . . D . . . C . . . G . . . B . . .

A . . . D . . . C . . . G . . . E . . . . *[C–G, G–B, and A–D are creative leaps.]* Don't you think you'll enjoy working this way? I love it, myself.

And now, let's put the D here, so we can finish that exercise. And the D wanted to go *[indicating the directions from D]*—was that right? *[sings]:* E–D–E', E–D–C, E–D–B. All right, so let's make our creative leap to D. Play and hold the E: E . . . and we'll leap together— on one mountain crag: E . . . D . . . B . . . E' . . . *[adding rhythmic variety]* C . . . D . . . B . . . D . . . A . . . B . . . F . . . G . . . E . . . . So having explored the directions of D after that creative leap, we made another leap from D to A, again explored its directions, and finally returned to our tonic tone. So there we had two creative leaps, and in between we worked with the natural directions, the natural dynamics that live in each tone.

I think this is enormously exciting! I think this opens up a whole new technique of improvisation. Just play the Phrygian E, the tonic: E . . . using this same technique of the octave in the left hand, the single tone in the right hand—now just do a little improvisation in that scale: *[Jean improvises.]* . . . Very nice! Now you can add rhythmic variety to that. This has a tremendous—really—it has a reality; and for the child, you are giving him a musical experience. How often do you feel, particularly in the first days of therapy, "Is what I'm giving this child a musical experience? Is what I am playing meaningful? Does it carry any of the truth of music that could awaken this Music Child we're always talking about?"

Okay. That's the message for today.

EDITOR'S NOTE   *The schema of tonal directions produced by this exploration continued to evolve in Exploration Three. A more developed schema incorporating these and still later clarifications is given at the end of that exploration, pages 30–31.*

In answer to a student's concern that such an analysis of melodic movement threatened to inhibit spontaneity and creativity in improvisation, Paul Nordoff emphasized that this approach to exploring and diagramming the inherent melodic tendencies of tones was essentially a study device aimed at focusing attention on the dynamics of tonal movement and enhancing awareness of them. It was never intended to produce a formula for melodic construction, but to provide a springboard for living, creative work. "What we need in therapy is the instant feeling in our fingers for the tonal-melodic dynamics of the tones we are using." As with most aspects of music, the realities of melodic expression are so livingly variable, complex, and subtle—see, for example, the later explorations of the inherent qualities of intervals—that they inevitably elude any attempt to encompass them in an analytically derived schema, and Nordoff was well aware of this.

It was also suggested that the technique of using tonal directions as an improvisational resource could be helpful to a therapist when he or she felt "dried up," or did not know musically what to do next. "It could be used at such moments, but it would have to be done with musical consciousness, with this kind of tonal perception. Then a therapist would not just be doodling, but working deliberately, and with a musical reality."

In answer to a student's question, Paul Nordoff also suggested: "Although we can't in therapy sing every tone before playing it, I do recommend it as a helpful exercise in practicing improvisation."

EXPLORATION THREE
TONAL DIRECTIONS AND CREATIVE LEAPS IN POLYPHONY AND HOMOPHONY

*T*he directional tendencies of tones in the scale; their application to all diatonic scales, in both ascending and descending movement. Illustrations of how clearly they are evident in Bach fugue subjects. Harmonic functions of supporting and influencing tonal directions in homophony, in which a single melody has harmonic accompaniment. An example of the synthesis of tonal directions and harmonic progression in a prelude by Debussy. The tradition in counterpoint of a leap being followed by a compensating melodic movement in the opposite direction, as evident in Bach fugue subjects. An illustration of the striking effects that can result when this principle is not followed. Tonal directions in several voices creating a harmonic progression, as exemplified in the writing of Wagner.

DIRECTIONS OF TONES, REVIEWED

Now, tell me again from your notes of yesterday: of course, the primary tone of the scale can go anywhere, can't it? The second tone, we found could go—tell me from your notes—up to three or back to one. *[With the students prompting, the tonal directions are written out.]* The third one of the scale could go up to four, back to two—and I think we made a mistake and missed something—three can also go to one. Four, we've found out again, can move up to five, down to three, two, and one. That covers it, does it? Five will have many possibilities. It goes to eight—yes, six, four, three, one. And six pulls toward seven, it pulls toward five, four, and three. Seven pulls toward eight, six, and five. I think that about covers it.

	E	F	G	A	B	C	D	E'
Ascending Inherent Directions	*Anywhere*	*G*	*A*	*B C*	*C E'*	*D*	*E'*	
Scale tones	E	F	G	A	B	C	D	E'
Descending Inherent Directions		*E*	*F E*	*G F E*	*A G E*	*B A G*	*C B*	

FIGURE 3-1.

Jean:	Would you call it a creative leap if four goes to seven?
Paul:	Four to seven? I think it would, Jean.
Jenny:	I do!
Paul:	I don't think it lies in the pull of the tone to go to seven. I think that would be a creative leap.

Well now, I have thought about this a little further: of course, one can also go down the scale, and then the same principles will apply, whether you are ascending or descending. You understand that.

I had the idea for doing this from the book *Sound and Symbol* by Victor Zuckerkandl. But in this book he takes the scale, and says that from the first tone to the fifth, every tone wants to go back, and from the fifth on, every tone wants to go on to the octave. In a sense that is true if you are playing the scale itself. But if you are thinking, as we are, in terms of the importance of each tone of the scale in its relationship to all the others, then this scheme simply doesn't work. But it was the germ of an idea for me. It is still a very valuable book; I'm not criticizing it at all, it's a wonderful book.

TONAL DIRECTIONS AND CREATIVE LEAPS IN BACH FUGUE SUBJECTS

[A number of melodic lines are written out. They are Bach fugue subjects from The Well-Tempered Clavier, *Book 1. The tonal relationships in their melodic movements are examined:]*

(1)

We start on the tonic, we go down to the seven—that's a natural direction of the tonic. Then we have seven going to three (1); that's really a creative leap, isn't it? But the rest of the melody follows the natural pull of the tone. To make this even more creative, as we're in C-sharp minor, the seventh is a B♯. Now this is the shortest fugue theme Bach ever wrote; it has only four different tones. Can we sing it? *[Supported by the piano, the students sing the first five tones.]* . . . It's so creative, it's hard to sing, isn't it!

It is a double fugue:

EXAMPLE 3-1. J.S. Bach, *Fugue* from *The Well-Tempered Clavier*, Book 1, no. 4.

[Playing the first nine measures]. . . . Just absolutely magnificent! It simply is following these wonderful directions of the tones, with one creative leap that brings the whole thing to life and opens it up.

You will find in the themes of the Bach fugues the most beautiful illustrations of the principle we were working with yesterday *[Exploration Two]*. Here's another one:

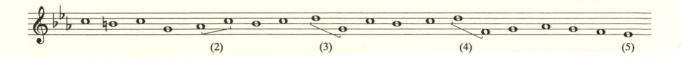

Now, there you see, this time, no creative leaps to begin with. We start with the tonic going down to the seventh and right back. And then from the C to the fifth note of the scale, and the fifth note has this wonderful direction to the sixth. Here the sixth note moves to the tonic, so there's a creative leap there (2). Then there's a repetition of the first three notes, and this time the tonic note C moves up to D. D does not go back to C, D does not go up to E♭, D makes a beautiful creative leap down to the G (3). Then we go back and repeat the first three notes again. We go up to D again, but the second note of the scale is not permitted to go in its natural directions, to three or to one, but leaps down to the fourth tone (4), a creative leap. From here on, we get the natural pull of each tone to one of its neighbors.

Shall we sing it? *[The fugue subject is sung slowly to a harmonic accompaniment that emphasizes the creative leaps.]* . . . That marvelous thing there (3) . . . ! At the end, how beautifully it comes to rest as each tone just takes its neighboring tone (5). And when you get that:

EXAMPLE 3-2. J.S. Bach, *Fugue* from *The Well-Tempered Clavier*, Book 1, no. 2.

. . . *[playing from the opening into the third measure]* . . . in the fugue itself, you're really playing with dynamite. It's so creative, it's so living!

Clive: This is a new way of understanding fugues, isn't it!
Paul: Ah! It's simply wonderful, and it carried us through the whole polyphonic movement—and applies all the way to every voice, to everything that's happening. Now, here's a very short one in contrast:

Here again, there is this beautiful creative leap from the second tone of the scale down to the fifth (6). But from here, it just moves quite beautifully from one neighboring tone—following the directions—from one neighboring tone to another.

This fugue, I think, has one of the most beautiful preludes of any of the forty-eight. Oh, Bach wrote so beautifully in triplets. It's the one that begins:

EXAMPLE 3-3. J.S. Bach, *Prelude* from *The Well-Tempered Clavier*, Book 1, no. 9, opening.

. . . [*playing the first one and one-half measures; repeating the first four tones of the first measure*]. . . . The melody follows the line of the chord, and the chord itself is following the directions of tones [*playing first three and one-half measures, bringing out the melody in the left hand, then accenting the dissonant interval E–D♯ (7) at the third beat of the fourth measure*]. . . . [*This analysis implies that the movement to the fifth is also to be heard as a natural direction of the third.*]

Let's sing the fugue. [*Supported by the melody on the piano, the students sing the tones of the subject as written.*] . . . And the rhythm!

EXAMPLE 3-4. J.S. Bach, *Fugue* from *The Well-Tempered Clavier*, Book 1, no. 9.

. . . *[playing into the second measure]*. Simply superb! The whole thing *[repeating the opening phrase]* . . . gets its marvelous life first from that rest, and then from the creative leap (6) from the second down to the fifth.

The last example I have for you follows completely without any creative leaps, follows completely the tonal directions, and yet I think it is one of the most beautiful themes he has ever written. *[The view that all intervals from the tonic were inherent directions was reconsidered in later explorations, and an ascending leap from the tonic to the sixth, as in this example Ab to F (8), came to be recognized as a creative leap. It certainly carries this feeling in this melodic line:]*

[The class sings the subject of J.S. Bach, Fugue *from the* Well-Tempered Clavier, *Book 1, no. 17.]* . . . Isn't it beautiful! Absolute simplicity! Absolutely beautiful. This wonderful sensitivity that every great composer has had to the directions, the forces, the active tonal impulses that live in the scale in which he is working—it's simply a marvelous thing to experience. I also suggest that you look at the F-sharp minor and the B-flat minor themes in Volume Two. Oh, any of them, they're all wonderful, but those two are particularly interesting.

HOMOPHONY: THE INFLUENCES OF HARMONY UPON TONAL DIRECTIONS

Then, you see, when you get to the time of homophony—one melody with a harmonic accompaniment—the eighteenth century onward, then you find the harmony beginning to enhance these directions of the single tone, to intensify them—enhance the directions, intensify the directions, anticipate the directions, support the directions. So these are functions of harmony that soon we will be studying—

Clive: Why don't you write that down? That's a marvelous set of thoughts!
Paul: Yes. How the harmony then can:

> *support* the tonal directions,
> *anticipate* tonal directions,
> *intensify* tonal directions, and
> *enhance* them.

It can also *conclude* them—you get this in the cadences, don't you?—where the harmony helps the tonal direction in its conclusion. So it helps also to conclude, to finish, to end a tonal direction. Beautiful functions of harmony that are so seldom touched upon and understood. It is only, all too often, taught as a separate part of the theory of music. This is a revelation, really.

I'd like to play you a little bit of Debussy, just to illustrate this. This is from one of the Preludes, called "Some Steps in the Snow":

EXAMPLE 3-5. Debussy, *Prelude*, Book 1, no. 6, "Des Pas sur la Neige."

It's in D minor, and it begins in a very strange rhythm . . . *[playing the left-hand opening]*. . . . He has taken the second in the direction of the third (9). . . . The melody begins (10) *[playing the tones rising along their tonal directions]* . . . ah! we've concluded (11) *[plays the falling phrase and, in measure four, the descending third, C–A]*. . . . There's a beautiful conclusion of the tonal direction in the D-minor triad (12). . . .

And now . . . *[the harmonies support the tonal direction of the melody (13)]* . . . anticipation! The harmony adds anticipation to the melodic movement (14) . . . he takes it still further (15). . . .

[Playing the next measure] . . . now, completely different harmony accompanying the first tonal movement (16) *[the second moving to the third]* which dominates the piece throughout. Marvelous, isn't it! And how these (17) . . . single tones . . . come after the chord each time . . . and the D going to the E. . . . It's held (18) . . . and then one falls *[descending phrase, seventh measure, right hand]*. . . .

A PRINCIPLE OF COUNTERPOINT DISREGARDED

Most often you will find a very interesting thing, which those of you who have studied counterpoint will know: when there has been a leap, the next movement is in the opposite direction to the leap.

If we look at the Bach fugue subjects: When there has been a leap, you see *[Example 3-1]*, (1) the melody moves in the opposite direction to the leap. Here again *[Fugue no. 17 on page 27], (19) and (8), it follows this principle beautifully [sings the phrase].*

So that part of the beauty of this is the fact that we are always moving in the opposite direction from the leap. The same thing here in Fugue no. 2 *[Example 3-2],* we leap down (3), we go up; we leap down (4), we go up.

Now, when this particular rule is not followed, some very exciting things can happen. For instance, let's sing this:

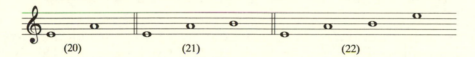

. . . Sol–do *[leading the singing from the piano]* (20) . . . and now the second tone of the scale (21). . . . We've skipped, we haven't gone back, we've gone up. Let's sing it again (21) . . . and now we're going to skip again *[singing (22) . . . and leading directly into]:*

EXAMPLE 3-6. Rouget de Lisle, *La Marseillaise.*

. . . one of the most stirring national anthems in the world, isn't it! It just goes this way! It just uplifts you. It doesn't go like that: *[miming solemnity]*, or like this: *[pomposity]*, it goes like this: *[call to action]!* And everyone gets on his feet! All of these things are very exciting.

TONAL DIRECTIONS IN HARMONIC WRITING

I think it would be a marvelous thing for us to sing this—you know, you can go back and back again to the same things and find more and more in them—this beautiful opening of *Tristan.*
    [The group is divided into the four parts.]

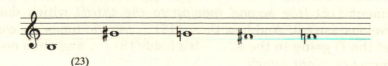

Let the middle voices begin. *[Led by the piano, the alto voices sing their part.]* . . . You see, *[playing the illustration]* that voice makes this beautiful creative leap (23) . . . and then comes back in half tones. May we sing it once more? . . . Now, I want the high voices. Come in when I do, *[to the altos]* . . . you'd better take a breath after that G♯.

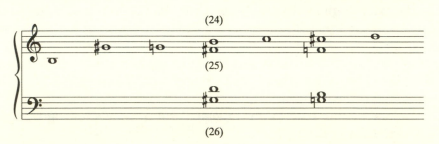

EXAMPLE 3-7. Wagner, *Tristan und Isolde*, opening (transposed one tone higher).

. . . *[the soprano voices are added, then the tenor and bass parts until all the parts are sung, with piano accompaniment].* . . . It is so beautiful! What is happening? This B (24) in the soprano voice is simply ascending in half tones. . . . The D (25) . . . in the tenor voice is finding its direction a third below *[the alto voice]*; the G♯ (26) . . . in the bass is being pulled down to the G♮, which is a memory of the . . . first tones in the descending line in the alto voice. So there's an echo in the bass of what happened in the very first tones. A wonderful experience to hear music this way, to feel music this way.

Knud: Let's do it again, shall we?
Students: Yes! *[The phrase is repeated.]* . . .
Tom: Once more for me! *[The phrase is repeated with instruction for the bass to pick up the G♯ from the alto part.]* . . .
Paul: It's like someone doing this *[feeling out before him as if in the dark]*, sleepwalking, almost, not really seeing. It's the whole mood of Isolde in that one phrase.
Clive: And there's the falling tragedy, the tragedy is implicit there.
Paul: The tragedy is all there in that first phrase. Everything that is going to happen is right there: love and death. It's really marvelous.

EDITOR'S NOTE

This exploration confirmed much of the schema of inherent tonal directions, and also expanded it and differentiated some of its fundamental elements:

The melodic dynamics of scale tones, identified in the Phrygian scale in Exploration Two, appear to be applicable to all diatonic scales.

The exploration began by considering the inherent directions of tones in the Phrygian scale within one octave. However, it is also necessary to consider descending directions from the lower tonic, and skipping or leaping from tones above this to tones below it. This will naturally increase the number of directions ascribed to the lower tonic and to some lower scale tones. Similarly, identifying inherent directions ascending from the upper tonic, and skipping or leaping from tones below it to tones above it, also adds to the directional possibilities of a number of upper scale tones.

The inherently natural directions of the tonic appear to be to all tones up to and including the dominant above, and down to and including the dominant below. Skips from the tonic beyond the dominant in either direction are considered creative leaps.

The melodic character of a skip, that is, whether it is experienced as an inherent direction or as a creative leap, depends on its position in the scale; for example, in the Phrygian, 1 to 4 (E to A) is a natural direction, but 4 to 7 (A to D), the same interval, is experienced as a creative leap.

The inherent directional relationship existing between two given tones in the scale appears to hold good whether the melodic movement between them is ascending or descending. The same seems to hold true for some, but not all, creative leaps.

Incorporating the elaborations of the concept that occurred in Exploration Three and in later revisions, the schema, as far as it evolved in the course, would probably appear thus:

Ascending Inherent Directions	F G A B	G A	A B	B C	C E'	D	E' F'	F' G' A' B'
Scale tones	E	F	G	A	B	C	D	E'
Descending Inherent Directions	D C B	E D C	F E D	G F E	A G E	B A	C B	D C B

FIGURE 3-2.

EXPLORATION FOUR
THE LIFE OF THE INTERVALS

*V*ictor Zuckerkandl's imaginative thinking about tone. Singing and listening to
intervals. Studying intervals to discover a hidden aspect of music that very
largely determines its emotional effects on us. Illustrations of the use of a single
interval by different composers. Rudolf Steiner's concept of the intervals. Exercises for
becoming familiar with the intervals and increasing the awareness of their effects in
musical and therapeutic contexts.

ZUCKERKANDL'S IMAGINATIVE THINKING ABOUT MUSIC

I read something really quite remarkable in *Sound and Symbol* which was very thrilling to
me because there aren't many people who talk this way. One of the things Zuckerkandl says
is, "music is a miracle" (p. 6). In talking about tone, he says every tone is "an event" (p. 12).
Isn't that a wonderful concept! A tone is "an event," and a tone contains limitless
possibilities. "Musical tones are conveyors of forces. Hearing music means hearing an action
of forces" (p. 37).

This is beautiful thinking about music for music therapists. This is the way we must
think about music. Tones contain activity, and tones become active in melody and harmony.

EXPERIENCING INTERVALS

Sissel, would you help me? Would you just sing any tone on the vowel sound "ah" in a
comfortable register for you, and hold it.

Sissel:	*[sings D above middle C]*. . . .
Paul:	Good! Tom would you sing another tone, related to this, the first one that comes to your mind.
Tom:	*[sings A♭ at the bottom of the bass clef]*. . . .
Paul:	Mm, would you sing them together?
Sissel and Tom:	*[sing the interval of an octave and a tritone]*. . . .
Paul:	OK. Amanda, would you sing a tone?
Amanda:	*[sings first space F♯]*. . . .
Paul:	Nancy, sing one, first one that comes to your mind. . . .
Nancy:	*[sings middle C♯]*. . . .
Paul:	Together.
Amanda and Nancy:	*[sing a perfect fourth]*. . . .
Paul:	Beautiful! *[plays the interval on the piano]*. . . .

[Following, as requested, and singing in turn:]

Jenny and Jean:	*[respectively: D below the treble clef and second line G♯; together, a tritone]*. . . .
	Knud and Tom: *[E♭ and C in the bass clef, a minor third]*. . . .

Jane W. and Elaine: *[first space F, and A♭ at the top of the bass clef, a minor sixth].* . . .

Anna and Jane H.: *[middle C and third line B♭, a minor seventh].* . . .

Sybil and Amanda: *[E♭ and E at the bottom of the treble clef, a minor second].* . . .

Paul: All these different intervals! Each one had life, each one had vitality, each one had interest, each one had an emotional quality all of its own.

The study of the intervals is really a study of one of the secret aspects of music, one that is hidden within the music you hear. We respond differently to each interval, and our emotional response to the sum of the intervals we hear must be a very important component of the entire emotional effect that music has upon us.

Just to illustrate the possibilities—just a tiny few of the possibilities—let us take these two sounds *[B♭–D♭]* . . . the minor third. Now you can think of that as B♭–D♭, or A♯–C♯. Let's think of it as B♭, and we find:

(1)

EXAMPLE 4-1. J.S. Bach, *Prelude* from *The Well-Tempered Clavier,* Book 2, no. 22, opening.

. . . we hear them (1), then, in the context of that beautiful B-flat minor prelude of Bach . . . there they are. . . . They immediately set up movement, expectation, mood, quality—the things that live in just this beginning in which that one interval, those two tones, are prominent.

Let's take them in another piece:

EXAMPLE 4-2. Schumann, *Phantasiestücke,* op. 12, "Aufschwung" (Soaring).

. . . there they are . . . in the accompanying figure there *[right hand]* . . . and the left hand moves from one to the other. . . . Completely different context, completely different use. The tones are the same.

Let us separate them, *[B♭]* . . . call it A♯:

EXAMPLE 4-3. Chopin, *Nocturne in F-sharp Major,* op. 15, no. 2.

. . . another completely different experience. There's one tone . . . *[in the right hand]*, the other is going to join it *[left hand (2)]*, in the Chopin nocturne. . . .

Now listen to how they occur in a minuet by Ravel:

EXAMPLE 4-4. Ravel, *Menuet* from *Sonatine,* opening.

. . . there they are (3). . . . They begin a second phrase; they indicate a new key. Again, there is movement, there is expectation. At the same time, it makes continuity with what has happened before. So we hear them now in a completely new context, a completely new mood, a completely different use of the same two notes.

And I'll play them this way *[B♭ and C♯, two octaves and a minor third apart]* . . . anything can happen!

EXAMPLE 4-5. Schumann, *Davidsbündler*, op. 6, no. 9, opening.

. . . now we have B♭ and C♯ *[playing the example]*. . . . That was Schumann's starting point, and you don't know what key you are in. Tonality has loosened up and we are in a completely new world of musical experience with the same two notes.

This is what you are bringing children: musical experience, through the meaningfulness of the intervals you use; the intention with which you use them; the activity the intervals set up, both tonal and rhythmic; the moods that can be established with them.

We can take these same two tones *[beginning to improvise]*:

EXAMPLE 4-6. Improvised example in a pentatonic scale.

. . . and go right off into the pentatonic scale, which again is not only a completely different experience in quality and mood, in activity, but a completely different experience within the context of the other tones that you are using—and an experience of an *idiom*.

So that to my mind, one of the most important series of exercises in "Developing Musical Resources" *[Part Five of* Creative Music Therapy*]* is the quite long list of exercises called "Harmonic Intervals: Differentiation of Their Sounds and Qualities." And here we are thinking in terms of harmonic intervals, naturally, of the two tones being played together *[C–C♯]*. . . .

STEINER'S INTERVAL CONCEPT

Those of you who have been in the recent course in Norway know the concept of the intervals that I mentioned that can be found in the lectures Rudolf Steiner gave to eurythmists. Eurythmy is an art of using movement, and these lectures concerned eurythmy to tone, to music. This is the concept, and I think it's enormously helpful and very provocative.

[Playing and holding middle C] . . . in the single tone we have absolute rest *[playing C]*. . . . We can experience this inwardly. I am sure you would agree with me that you could not consider this *[C]* . . . as an outer experience in which you are active outside of yourself, or active *[C]* . . . in relationship to something outside of yourself. You are really, in a single tone *[C],* . . . enclosed, and this is an inner experience.

But with the minor second *[playing C–D♭ as a harmonic interval]* . . . something begins to move. But you are still within yourself. This is an inner movement *[repeating C–D♭]* . . . an inner activity *[playing the minor second F–G♭ . . . then D–E♭]*. . . .

But with the major second *[playing D–E]* . . . the activity increases. *[From this point onward Paul Nordoff bases his explanation of widening intervals on the tone D.]* Curiously enough, *[returning to D–E♭]* . . . this is the beginning of activity, of inner movement; *[playing D–E]* . . . this is carrying that inner movement still further. And it is asking *[D–E]* . . . for something. This movement, this disturbance, wishes to find *[playing the minor third D–F]* . . . rest.

It finds it in the minor third, which is *[D–F]* . . . still an inner experience *[D–F]* . . . but now it is an experience of inner balance *[D–F]*. . . . The movement has paused, both in the minor *[D–F] third* . . . which has its particular quality as it is still leaning [D–E] . . . back toward the second from which it came. *[D–F]*. . . . But the major third no longer leans back *[playing the major third D–F♯]*. . . . It is a very positive statement of inner balance *[D–F♯]*. . . . And it's very interesting that our harmonic system is based entirely on this interval in which *[D–F♯]* . . . this balance was felt. And music comes from within *[D–F♯]*. . . . The whole development of music has been through an expression of the human being in tone: an expression of himself.

With the fourth *[playing the perfect fourth D–G]* . . . again there is movement, inner movement *[D–G]* . . . but it is reaching further toward the outside. It is taking the first *[D–G]* . . . step toward an outer relationship—it's not there yet.

And *[playing the tritone D–G♯]* . . . with this most mysterious of all the intervals, the augmented fourth, the tritone, with this *[D–G♯]* . . . beautiful interval, we have the possibility *[playing the perfect fourth D–G]* . . . of withdrawing *[playing the major third D–F♯]* . . . and of sinking further back into ourselves.

We also *[D–G♯]* . . . have the possibility of taking a step *[playing the perfect fifth D–A]*. . . . And in taking the step to the fifth, we are now facing outer experience. We can think now *[D–A]* . . . of the emotional content of the fifth as being a standing in balance *[D–A]* . . . facing the experiences with which we can relate ourselves *[D–A]*. . . .

And then we take a deep breath and *[the minor sixth D–B♭]* . . . move out! We are no longer within ourselves. We are now putting out a hand to this world of *[D–B♭]* . . . sight, of sound, of human relationship, of tonal relationship.

With the interval of the major sixth *[D–B]* . . . we move out more actively *[D–B]* . . . we are carried out into the world *[D–B]* . . . we step into the external world.

With the minor seventh *[D–C]* . . . we now begin to feel a tension between us and what is outside of us *[D–C]*. . . .

And with the major seventh *[D–C♯]* . . . this tension reaches its highest point. It's wonderful that in eurythmy *[D–C♯]* . . . the gesture you make for seventh has the arms extended above the head with the hands quivering. It's a wonderful expression of this feeling of the seventh, and of being *outside [D–C♯]*. . . .

And with the octave *[D–D']* . . . wow! You've caught your ego in its relationship to outer experience.

THE CHARACTER OF THE OCTAVE

So an octave is *never* just a doubling of the same tone eight tones higher. The octave is an *ego experience*. We don't play octaves in a random way; we don't play octaves to double a tone. We play octaves because we are bringing to the children an ego experience in tone *[improvising]*:

EXAMPLE 4-7. Improvisation using octaves.

If I did that in a single tone *[improvising]*:

EXAMPLE 4-8. Improvisation using single-tone melody.

. . . it's not the same thing at all. . . . And I'm not merely "doubling" here *[returning to Example 4-7]* . . . I'm bringing another dimension into the musical experience by playing this in octaves.

Sybil: Now you have explained to me why I found the exercise in which you play your right hand in single notes and your left hand in octaves (or vice versa)—this is such a simple thing—to be enormously effective. I had been wondering why.

Paul: Yes. Well, that's why. I think this is a very beautiful concept; a very telling concept; a deeply spiritual concept; and a concept that relates us to tone.

Jenny: It's been, for me, a very moving experience going through them like that, feeling the opening out.

Paul: It's a wonderful experience. It's beautiful to bring children interval experiences that move out and withdraw, because this is another use of the principle of tension and relaxation, which they now are getting tonally.

We want the children to have as much musical-tonal experience as possible to accompany their drum beating, because drum beating is not *just* drum beating. When a child is joyfully beating the basic beat to the music you improvise, he is beating the music you improvise. He is not beating a drum; he is beating *music*. This is what many people will have to learn: that drum beating is not a primitive experience. The idea of primitive experience is ridiculous anyway, because we know enough now to know that the music of so-called primitive people is very complicated indeed. Some of it is highly sophisticated, beautifully organized. So there is no such thing as primitive drum beating. The drum beating of Indians, for instance, is simply fantastic. The drum beating of Africans as well.

Jenny: Paul, may I say just one more thing? It's very interesting, this idea of the major third being a positive statement of inner balance. Isn't it significant that this was first used in our harmony at the time of the Renaissance, when man was refinding himself! It came with that development in his relationship to himself. This was the crucial interval of the Renaissance music.

Paul: This was the crucial interval. And never forget that when this interval first appeared, there was a Papal Bull—

Jenny: Against it!

Paul: —against it.

Jenny: Absolutely.

Paul: It was used first in secular music and then was finding its way into the church. This fundamental and beautiful third, which has been exteriorized into a harmonic system, is something that lives in us as an experience of inner balance. And who is balanced? Douglas, when he rocks, is in a state of beautiful inner balance. So I play *[D]* . . . and he sings *[singing F♯]* . . . it just expresses what he's doing. He is living within himself. *[See editor's note on page 41 for background on Douglas.]*

Clive: He's not in the fifth, he's in the third.

Paul: He is happy in this, he's at rest in this, and so he sings. He expresses his inner state by singing the third.

PRACTICING EXPERIENCING INTERVALS

So when you have differentiated the intervals and played them many times, play a number of each one. Play a number of minor seconds, of major seconds, of minor thirds, and so on. Play them at random, but listen to them. Become aware of their differences. Form them on different tones; play them freely on any tone. Then begin to play freely, different intervals on any tone:

EXAMPLE 4-9. Improvised example using succession of harmonic intervals.

. . . and you will become more and more aware of the wonders that lie in the qualities of each one, and of the fact that each one has its own emotional quality. It doesn't need to be described. I don't have to ask you what this makes you think of *[playing the minor second A–Bb]* . . . that would take us into a world we're not concerned with at all. We're only concerned with the pure experience of it, the pure sound of it, the pure quality of it.

Knud: So you want us, when we play different intervals, just to take an interval and listen, not to think in advance?

Paul: Not to think in advance—unless you want to. Unless you think *[playing the fourth C–F]* . . . "I want to hear the fourth" *[C–F]*. . . . You can think that much, certainly. "And another fourth *[Ab–Db]*. . . . Now, how will a major seventh sound in contrast *[F–E]* . . . to this? And a minor second in contrast *[A–Bb]* . . . to that? And an octave *[G–G']* . . . ?"

Clive: Oh that's wonderful! *[The students agree.]*

Paul: Beautiful! The purity of the octave! If you have ever experienced a balance between you and something outside of yourself, in a moment of human relationship, or in a moment of realizing that this flowering hawthorn is one of the most beautiful things God ever made *[playing the octave G–G']* . . . this expresses it. There you are, and there it is, and you are together. You have become it, and it is a part of you. That's all expressed in this octave. Then, when you get into using the intervals in octaves, you will have a completely different experience:

EXAMPLE 4-10. Improvisation using harmonic intervals with the lower tone in octaves.

Jean, there was one moment in your session today when you hadn't been playing with your left hand, and you brought in an octave in your left hand that made a dissonance of beautiful quality with what had gone on before. It was very striking. Do you remember that? It was something worth repeating. If you can dig that out of the tape recording and note it, it could be something well worth repeating.

We mustn't be afraid to repeat. We're bringing the child experiences—tonal experiences—he has not had before, certainly not used in this way. We want to make them part of him. We want to bring him to feeling that these express him, that these communicate something from you to him. Don't forget, the therapist is communicating, or should be, to the child. He's communicating whatever he has to communicate through music: his care for the child, his acceptance of the child, his interest in the child, his respect for the child. All of this can be communicated through the music you make with and for the child.

BECOMING AWARE OF THE LIFE OF THE INTERVALS IN A COMPOSITION

But just to touch very briefly on what goes on in any piece of music you might hear—that you are not aware of—I always like to use, as it's slow and illustrative, the slow movement of the Beethoven "Pathétique":

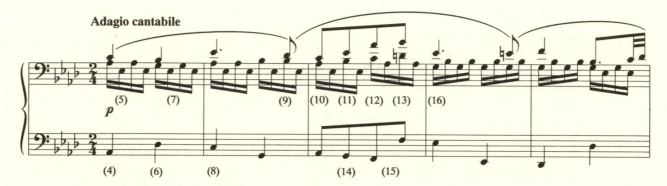

EXAMPLE 4-11. Beethoven, *Piano Sonata in C Minor,* op. 13, "Pathétique," second movement, opening.

Now it starts (4) . . . with a major third here . . . with an octave . . . and this low A♭ . . . also supports the tenth. . . . With the very second note (5) . . . the whole picture changes. We have now a fifth . . . and we have a sixth. . . . *[repeats].* . . . Do you feel that change? And now (6) . . . ooh! Something fantastic has happened. We have . . . the tritone, we have a minor third . . . and we have a major sixth. . . . Again (7) . . . the E♭ comes and changes everything . . . takes away the tritone, leaves a major second and a fifth. . . . *[repeating the first measure and stopping on (8)]* . . . and then we have the fifth. Another world!

We're responding to these subconsciously all the time. The sum total of this is the sum total of our musical-emotional experience as we are listening to it. I've only played three beats of it and what has happened? Everything!

Look at it again. We have begun in a period of balance (4). . . . We have withdrawn (6). . . . At the same time in this . . . there's the possibility of moving out . . . and we move out (8) . . . we now have the fifth and minor sixth . . . .[1] We withdraw again into the minor third (9). . . . Now the intervals in the right hand open out, chord by chord—major third (10) . . . fourth (11) . . . minor sixth (12) . . . minor sixth (13)—which give this rising melodic line, while the left hand . . . reinforces this moving out with its stepwise contrary motion (14) . . . only to leap up an octave with the climax of the melody (15). . . . This last chord in the third measure modulates to the dominant on the first beat of the fourth measure, where we can pause. . . . We have come to the interval of sixth (16) . . . we have taken a step outside

[1] Listeners to the CD recording of this exploration will find that the analysis given in the remainder of the paragraph is not on the recording. The text given here is taken from a later unrecorded discussion.

ourselves and we now pause . . . secure in the root position dominant chord—in a sixth, supported by the balance of the third beneath. . . .

What a *privilege* to be able to play it; to be able to listen to it!

Now do you know why I said last week that music is a miracle? Why this wonderful guy in Germany *[Zuckerkandl]* says music is a miracle? It is a miracle! And we're working with miracles. And things happen to children in music that don't happen any other place.

Now, when you learn new pieces with your teachers, or when you study a piece of music, look at what's happening. Look at the life of the intervals as they weave and interweave, and change and work, and bring constantly new emotional experience into our lives. Become aware of this. This is the touchstone. This is a hypostasis, a foundation for the work we want to do.

Okay, we're off!

This is what I mean by looking at music in new ways so that our therapy will be creative and true.

EDITOR'S NOTE   *The reference to Douglas on page 38 is to a clinical study presented previously in the course, and described in Nordoff, P., and Robbins, C.,* Therapy in Music for Handicapped Children, *under the pseudonym "Russell."*

Douglas began music therapy in a day-care unit for young psychotic children at the age of three and one-half. He was totally lacking in speech and displayed typical autistic behaviors: avoiding all contact and rejecting changes in routine or environment. On being brought to the music room, he would climb hurriedly on a chair, fold his legs under him, and become involved in a continuous forward and backward rocking, grunting—at first in protest—as he rocked forward. He was skillful at pitching his weight in his rocking and could propel the heavy, solid chair backward on the smooth floor. At first, he began every session by doing this to put a distance between himself and the therapist. His music was mostly played and sung in the style of a Gregorian chant, and in the rhythm of his rocking and grunting. Quite quickly, his sounds of protest would shift into the key of the music and he would sing strong, sustained tones, then he would pitch his weight differently in his rocking and move his chair forward, until he was sitting, rocking-grunting-singing close beside the therapist. Much of his music was in D, and because of its chantlike quality, Douglas would often be presented with the open fifth D–A, repeated rhythmically, accompanying his rocking. It was remarkable how, on several occasions, he vocally put in the third by holding a strong F♯ as he rocked.

EXPLORATION FIVE
THE INTERVAL CONCEPT AND THE POTENTIAL
IN THE SINGLE TONE

Rudolf Steiner's psychospiritual concept of the intervals in their relationship to human experience; the applicability of this universally important concept to therapy. Zuckerkandl's view of the dynamic potential of the single tone and its important implications for therapy. Examples of compositions with very different characters that open with the same single tone. The living application of these concepts to improvisation and therapy.

THE INTERVAL CONCEPT AND ITS APPLICATION TO THERAPY

Do not lose sight of the concept of the intervals that I gave you from Rudolf Steiner's lectures to the eurythmists *[Exploration Four]*. This is a universal, not a personal, concept. And this you can *definitely* use with children. You might yourself have completely different experiences with the intervals, or you might describe them in different ways. But taking this as a basic fundamental human concept—a psychospiritual one, if you like—you will find that you can use this directly in therapy. We can show you examples of this on many tapes: the particular effects that the particular intervals have had that are absolutely in accordance with this concept.

THE POTENTIAL OF THE SINGLE TONE

Now to go on with the intervals: we can't, of course, ever lose sight of the single tone, because an interval is composed of two of these. As you remember, we spoke of tones as events, as forces, depending upon how they are used, where they occur, and their position in the particular tonality that is being used. Again, I turn to this remarkable book *Sound and Symbol*, where Zuckerkandl says:

> . . . we can hear the very first tone of a composition as dynamically active as a musical tone, although dynamic quality is manifested as a relation *between* tones. We hear in it the *promise of a whole* that it bears within itself.[1]

This is a marvelous concept. The single tone holds within itself—and so many compositions begin with a single tone—"the promise of the whole" that is to come. The whole experience.

I have a few examples of this, just taking the tone B♭. One of the most striking and beautiful is:

---

[1] Page 37. Italics in the original.

EXAMPLE 5-1. Brahms, *Piano Concerto in B-flat Major*, op. 83, opening.

[Playing the first tone] . . . we'll just take the tone B♭. . . . *[playing the opening measure]* Something has begun . . . that beautiful horn solo that begins Brahms's *Second Concerto [playing the piano part in the second and third measures . . . then returning to the horn's B♭ and playing through the fourth and fifth measures].* . . . Again . . . and how beautifully, logically, naturally it moves between tonic and dominant, these fundamental, archetypal musical experiences to which we respond and will always respond.

Here's the same B♭:

EXAMPLE 5-2. J.S. Bach, *Prelude* from *The Well-Tempered Clavier*, Book 2, no. 22, opening.

. . . *[plays half the first measure]*. . . . Again, a completely new world has opened up from that same B♭. The whole that is to come lives within that first tone.

And:

EXAMPLE 5-3. Mozart, *Piano Sonata in E-flat Major*, K. 282, third movement, opening.

. . . *[playing the first two measures]* . . . the Mozart sonata. A repeated B♭, again, a completely different experience. *[Starting at the beginning again and playing through the eighth measure]*. . . . And this (1) is not just filling in the three beats, ta–ta–ta. *[repeating measures seven and eight]*. . . . What a wonderful gesture that octave is, what a wonderful movement that is between the melodic phrases—also on the B♭. So the B♭ contains all these worlds—all these possibilities—of modulation, of tonal relationship, of variation, of moods, of emotional experiences.

Listen, here's another B♭. . . . What is going to come out of this one?

EXAMPLE 5-4. J.S. Bach, *Chorale Prelude, "Sleepers Wake!"* (transcription by Myra Hess).

. . . . A wonderful chorale prelude of Bach: "Awake, the voice calls."

We must become very, very sensitive to each single tone as the possible bearer of a therapeutic music for this child. Then when we come to the harmonic combination of two tones sounding together, we have even more force, already, to begin with.

STUDYING, ABSORBING, AND APPLYING: THE LIVING PROCESS

Now, when you take these ideas and concepts away, don't try to use them immediately. Let them first become *yours*. Just as it would be impossible for a child who is just beginning to learn words to speak a scholarly sentence, it is impossible to do "the real thing," as Clive called it, in therapy with a new concept of the intervals when it is as new as this. Let it sink into you. You can't remember having learned to speak; you can't remember having learned to read or write; this is what should happen to the instruction you are getting here. It becomes part of your subconscious life, part of your subconscious abilities and equipment. Gradually, you will find *of itself* this comes into your improvisation and into your work. But you mustn't try to force it, or to use it intellectually, and you certainly mustn't be stopped by it.

EXPLORATION SIX
ELABORATION OF THE INTERVAL CONCEPT

*E*laboration of the interval concept with illustrations from Beethoven's Piano Sonata in E-flat Major, op. 81a, "Les Adieux." The sensitivity of Beethoven to the expressive dynamics of intervals. The movement from inner to outer, as mediated by the tensions of intervallic movement; how this movement mirrors life experience. The power and intervallic components of the diminished seventh chord. Analyzing intervallic movement. The value of playing intervals attentively, meditatively, as a way of becoming sensitive to their differences and expressive contents. The importance of imbuing music for therapy with a "breathing life"; the effect of silences in achieving this. Balance, space, and breathing as aspects of great music that can be used with therapeutic intent. An example of alternating intervals in Beethoven's Piano Sonata in E Major, op. 109. The great composers as guides, companions, and therapists; their music as therapy.

I was thinking that one of the secrets of the greatness of Beethoven is his marvelous sensitivity to the emotional content of the intervals, his sensitivity to their expressive force and expressive dynamic. The opening bars of the sonata "The Farewell, the Absence, and the Return" [*"Les Adieux"*] came into my mind.

EXAMPLE 6-1a. Beethoven, *Piano Sonata in E-flat Major,* op. 81a, "Les Adieux," opening to the eighth measure.

INNER BALANCE, TENSION, THEN RESOLUTION

Beginning with (1) . . . the major third, which, as you remember from our concept, is an inner experience of balance *[repeating the third]* . . . and moving from this to the fifth (2) . . . and you remember with the fifth we are standing, facing the world—and then . . . he takes a step further to the minor sixth (3). So beautiful. Still with the fifth beneath it *[C–G]* . . . so that you haven't gone very far, but you've taken a little step. You can see this as movement, from here (1) . . . to here (2) . . . and then (3) . . . the reaching out—but still with one foot on the fifth, so to speak.

And now the third (4) . . . begins to move toward a larger interval, a tritone (5) . . . *[playing the intervals in the left hand],* and it does . . . to the minor sixth (6), and this moves still further out to an augmented sixth (7) . . . and we're left with two octaves (8). . . .

Marvelous breathing in there, marvelous movement in there, from inner experience to outer experience through tension, which is a life experience. We're constantly doing this in our lives: moving from ourselves to something outside of ourselves. And if it has a real meaning, there is some tension in this movement from inner to outer.

[Returning to the sonata and beginning to play at measure four] . . . It's absolutely wonderful . . . contracting and resting again on the interval . . . of the major third (9), we also have the fourth . . . and we have the octave supporting this. . . .

[Playing the fifth measure] . . . He knows when to repeat things, too (10). . . . My composition teacher used to say "If it's good, repeat it; if it isn't worth repeating, throw it out!" *[The students laugh.]* And then . . . *[playing the sixth measure]* (12) . . . and then this (13). . . . What chord is that . . . ? The dominant seventh *[repeating the chord].* . . . It should go here, shouldn't it *[playing an E♭ major chord]* . . . ? That's the expectation it can arouse, but it goes there (14). . . .

THE DIMINISHED SEVENTH CHORD

This is one of the most powerful chords in music. Within the compass of the major sixth, B♭–G, *[at the blackboard]* we have three minor thirds that compose the diminished seventh chord. The minor third in itself is an inner experience, shading toward the second—not as far away from the second as the major third—shading toward the second, which is an experience of inner activity. So the rest in the minor third has just begun. We have three of these piled one on top of the other.

In addition there is the tritone in this chord, and this is an interval of tension. It has the tension of having moved beyond the fourth, which itself has moved out from the balance of the major third, and it has the tension before the step into the fifth. It can also withdraw into the fourth. So the tritone in itself contains musical force and tension, and here we have two of them.

Here we have a chord that you can really say is a chord of conflict. You have the sixth, which is a step outside of yourself. You have two tritones, which are steps toward facing the world. And you have this built by the superimposing of one minor third upon another. This is the tremendous power of this chord. One immediately feels it when Beethoven uses it here *[playing (13) . . . (14), then resolving to (15)]* . . . ah, thank God! So we go again to what? A dominant seventh, the same one that led to this *[repeating (14)].* . . . This resolves (15) . . . but do you go to E♭ major? No, indeed (16). . . . You go to a new world, a new world of tonal experience. And what do you have in that world? You have again the supporting octave (16) . . . the fifth . . . and the sixth. . . . A beautiful balance in octave, fifth, and sixth—as well, of course, as the tenth, which makes . . . the major third. So it's all there. *[repeating from (12) to (16)].* . . . The curtain goes up!

This is the beautiful sensitivity that Beethoven had for the tremendous emotional, expressive dynamics of the intervals. When you are practicing the interval exercises, I ask you to play each one, dwell on each one, meditate—in a way—on each one, to feel the difference, the content of each one.

We can all agree on this concept. I don't think there's anything in it to quarrel about. It's not as if I asked you what color does this remind you of *[playing a major third]*; you might say blue, another might say pink. It doesn't matter; we're not talking about colors, colors and music. We are using a concept that I think is meaningful for everyone, so in a sense it is universal. *[At this point the exploration was recessed, to be continued the next day.]*

ANALYZING INTERVALLIC MOVEMENT

Can we just go back to the Beethoven of yesterday? It haunted me in the night. The whole sonata came back to me, and I haven't looked at it for perhaps twenty years.

The directions which tones *of themselves* want to take: they set up a need that the next harmony should fulfill. And when Beethoven takes that dominant seventh somewhere else, it's immediately right, because the chord has resolved correctly, tonally we can accept it, and it sets up its need for what is to come.

I made a little sketch that I thought might be interesting for us all to have:

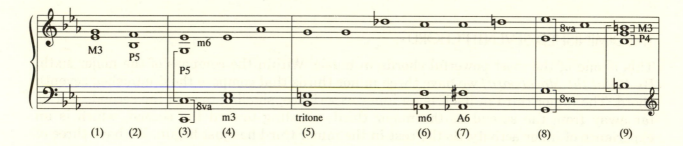

EXAMPLE 6-1b. Beethoven, *Piano Sonata in E-flat Major,* op. 81a, "Les Adieux," first eight measures, analysis of intervallic movement and the intervallic components of chords.

It's terribly hard to make schemes out of these things, really, but it is important that you see what's happening between the soprano voice, the bass voice, and the alto voice. We can't really go further with this. It would take too long and it's much too complicated. It's just a little tiny bit of a sketch to show you how you yourselves can begin to examine some of the music you're studying.

   [Playing the opening one and a half measures of the sonata]. . . . That really is a statement. You don't need to phrase it . . . you don't need to do this *[playing the phrase making a diminuendo];* that would be quite wrong. To make a crescendo *[demonstrating]* . . . wouldn't sound right either. Just the statement. And Beethoven has written the words "Le-be-wohl" . . . one syllable over each of the chords, "Live well." "Farewell."

   Now here is the octave . . . the minor third (3) . . . moving to the sixth (4). . . . And the minor third in the left hand—look . . . it opens to the tritone (5). . . . We keep that tension. . . . Now we have a sixth in the bass (6) . . . which opens to the minor seventh (7) *[written as an augmented sixth, A♭–F♯]* . . . then we get those wonderful two octaves (8), with just the interval of the sixth here *[playing G–E♭].* . . . Now, it builds . . . through a diminished seventh . . . and finishes on G–B–D (9), the dominant of C minor. C minor is the key.

   [Repeating the first measure] (1) . . . What could it be, (2) . . . what key? You really don't know. It could be E♭ major *[replacing (3) with an E♭ major chord].* . . .

   [Beginning the movement again . . . pausing at (9)] Now he repeats that an octave higher. . . . That's G major (10) . . . it goes to G minor (11) . . . a dominant (12) . . . tonic, dominant in E♭ (13). . . . *[plays (14)].* . . . Then comes this glorious diminished seventh . . . and the dominant in E♭ (15) . . . moving to this wonderful key (16).

continued on next page

continued from preceding page

EXAMPLE 6-1c. Beethoven, *Piano Sonata in E-flat Major,* op. 81a, "Les Adieux," *Adagio*
opening from measure eight into the beginning of the *Allegro* section.

So now we're in C♭ (17). . . . See the marvelous structure, this (18) is repeating that (17)
rhythmically with completely different tones. . . . Now what happens . . . ? *[completing the*
Adagio *section and commencing the first measure of the* Allegro*].* . . . Then the *Allegro* begins.
Those silences (19) in the last measures of the *Adagio* are simply fantastic, aren't they? The
music has a breathing life all of its own. There must be breathing life, too, in our music for
the children, so they feel this breathing life, this space, these silences . . . (20).

Clive: Sybil did that so well in her session yesterday. The music breathed, came
           to a beautiful pause—and then went on again. Really wonderful.
Paul: Yes, very fine.

Just let me play you just a little of the *Allegro.* We've started the sonata with the third (1). . . .
Now in the *Allegro,* we have a third right here (21) . . . and another . . . and another . . .
[indicating thirds in the left hand, then playing through (24)]. . . . Isn't that tremendous!
[repeating the C♭]. . . . What a difference between *[repeating (22) to (24) and substituting a*
C♮ *for the C♭]* . . . using the natural tone of the E♭ major scale! No, he had to have this (24) . . .
the tremendous tenseness and direction of the C♭ that absolutely must be followed by the B♭.
The breathing of . . . that octave (23) going up and coming down *[playing (22) to (23)]:* there's
a tremendous gesture that lives in this music.

DERIVING INSPIRATION FROM THE GREAT COMPOSERS

We can take these great things that live in great music as therapeutic goals, too. We want gesture in our music. We want space in it, we want breathing in it. We want the tones to go to the tones to which they're leading, or to tones that seem absolutely right for them to go to. Dah–*dah*–dah! (23). You couldn't do that octave any other way. You have to stretch for that, you have to reach up to heaven where it came from. That's a marvelous sonata.

So Beethoven's a good one to study for the sensitive use of intervals with an acknowledgment of their wonderful capacities for emotional expression.

INTERVALS IN ALTERNATION

Yesterday we were working with alternate intervals, which I thought was a very interesting tonal experience for everyone to have.

EXAMPLE 6-2. Beethoven, *Piano Sonata in E Major*, op. 109, opening.

[In this example, Paul Nordoff, continuing to work from memory, recomposes Beethoven. The intervals he refers to and plays as sixths are octaves in the original score.]
Beethoven takes *[playing the successive melodic intervals as harmonic intervals]* . . . a third (25) . . . followed by a fifth (26) . . . a fourth (27) . . . by a sixth (28) . . . a third (29) . . . by a fifth (30) . . . a fourth (31) by a sixth (32) . . . and he does: *[playing the piece as written, except for the octaves, to the cadence (33) in the fifth measure]*. . . . That's just so absolutely wonderful. He does it *[the pattern third–fifth–fourth–sixth]* . . . three times before the five-one (33). And he uses it *[playing from the first measure again]* . . . with all the tones rising, and then in the answering phrase they fall. . . .

Clive: It's so nice you invoke the great composers in this course!
Paul: Oh, the great composers must be with us. They must be our guides, and companions and friends, because think of the therapy they have done. My God! How many times have we really been miserable, and Bach has got us out of a slough of despond, or Beethoven has brought us just what we needed. Bach was always my therapy in times of depression.

EXPLORATION SEVEN
TRIADS AND INVERSIONS

*C*omparing triads in root position with inverted triads: root position triads as *"nouns," inverted triads as "verbs." The dynamics characteristics of sixth chords and six-four chords. Examples of composers' use of inversions. Doubling tones in root position triads and inversions; dispelling dogmatic rules. Suggestions for the use of inverted triads in therapy. Advice on practicing. Time in music therapy as "tonal" or "experiential" time. Renewing one's perception of all of music through music therapy.*

THE TRIAD IN THE ROOT POSITION

The triad itself we are too accustomed to take for granted. When I play this:

and the root is C *[playing a low C]*, . . . every C on the piano is the root of this chord. Every C in the world *[C]* . . . is the root of this triad at this moment *[playing the tones of the chord in sequence].* . . . The triad in the root position is affirmative, strong, declaring. I thought almost of saying it was like a noun. But the moment you invert the triad, you get verbs, you get movement. Something must happen.

THE INHERENT QUALITIES OF INVERSIONS

Without the inversions of triads, music as we know it, the music of the Western Hemisphere—of our civilization, if you want to call it that—would be absolutely impossible. In working with sixth chords and with six-four chords, we are not working with "just chords," because the sum of these three tones is far greater than any one of them taken individually. We're working with dynamic forces.

THE SIXTH CHORD

Just think, for instance, what a difference it makes to play a chord in root position and the same chord in sixth position:

EXAMPLE 7-1. Beethoven, *Piano Sonata in C Major*, op. 53, "Waldstein," opening.

. . . *[playing the first two measures, and stopping on the first beat of the third measure].* . . . That's a sixth chord *[emphasizing the bass note].* You start with the chord in the root position *[repeating the passage and stopping at the same point, again emphasizing the sixth chord]* . . . and you just feel the difference between the chord that is rooted on its tonic tone . . . and the chord that is now transformed—inverted—so that the third of the chord is in the bass.

In the music you study, in the music you practice, when you bring music to a child, be aware of the dynamic force that lives in the tones you are assembling, the tones you are presenting. These are the things that reach the child. It's not just a sound that reaches him, or a rhythm that reaches him, or the fact that you're accompanying him, or the fact that you're setting his beating to music. It is *how* you are doing it, and how you are using the material to accomplish what you want to do.

The very simplest position of the sixth chord just looks like nothing at all:

What is it? *[playing the chord . . . then immediately]:*

continued on next page

continued from preceding page

EXAMPLE 7-2. Beethoven, *Piano Sonata in C Major,* op. 2, no. 3, last movement, opening.

. . . they're all the sixth chord. That's what Beethoven could do with it. That's what *you* can do with it for a child! *[continues playing]:*

EXAMPLE 7-3. Improvisation using sixth chords in the style of the preceding example.

. . . . Marvelous sounds! Beautiful chords that keep the music in a certain elevation. The inversions arouse expectation, so that actually there is an element of tension in an inversion that does not exist in the chord in the root position. The inversions point, they lead. They have a direction.

INVERTED TRIADS

In *Creative Music Therapy,* *[in the chapter entitled]* "Musical Resources, Inverted Triads: Differentiation and Flexibility," beginning with exercise 21, the chords are in open position, and they sound well in open position. They sound well, for instance, in such a position as this:

. . . where the *[playing C]* . . . "sun" of the triad—the root—is doubled, and the "planets" are not *[repeating the chord]*. . . . However, it is quite possible that you would want to double the third. *[In a different instructional situation the students had been told that the third must never be doubled. Beginning to demonstrate]* . . . It's a marvelous sound:

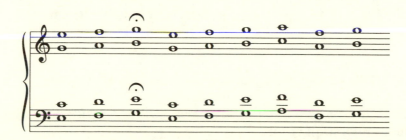

EXAMPLE 7-4. Open sixth chords with doubled third.

. . . and it's even possible that you might want to triple the third! A very beautiful example of that:

EXAMPLE 7-5. Beethoven, *Piano Sonata in D Minor*, op. 31, no. 2, "Tempest," opening.

. . . *[slowly arpeggiating the first chord and melodic tones]* . . . is the Beethoven sonata that starts on a sixth chord, and it has three thirds. The C♯ is there three times. *[playing through the* Allegro *and* Adagio *sections]*. . . . And he does it again *[arpeggiating the* Largo *chord in the seventh measure]*. . . . What a wonderful sound *[beginning to improvise]* . . . that would be:

EXAMPLE 7-6. Improvisation using sixth chords with thirds tripled.

. . . to give a child who's really using the "free arm swing,"[1] *really* beating the drum, *really* beating the cymbal, and you play him:

. . . sixth chords with three thirds. That's a marvelous sound.

    We can't make any dogmatic rules. Everything is possible, depending on the child, the moment, the situation, his response, what the music has led up to, your response to his response.

Alfred: An interesting thing is to be aware of the richness of that effect.
Paul: Not only the richness, Alfred, the power, the force, the dynamic forces
            that live in this tripled third. It's really greater than richness. It is so
            supportive. There's something magnificent about it.

Then, when we do such a simple thing as this:

---

[1] The "free arm swing" is a style of beating a drum or cymbal with large, free arm movements intended to loosen up a timid or constricted posture at the instruments, and to give a child a musically supported sense of expressive freedom and assertive confidence.

. . . we go into a completely different world. With just the change of one note, from this *[playing the sixth chord]* . . . to this *[playing the six-four chord]*. . . . Can you hear that . . . ?

Jane, come and play in the key of C any number of sixth chords—musically, meditatively, they're so beautiful.

Jane W.:   *[improvises]:*

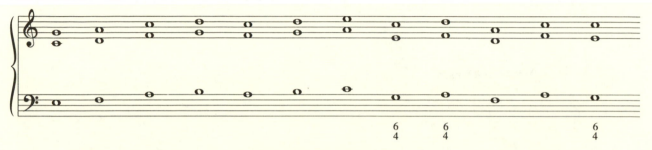

EXAMPLE 7-7. Improvisation based on sixth chords in the key of C, closing, by request, with a six-four chord.

. . . . That's it. Isn't that wonderful! Thank you, Jane.

THE SIX-FOUR CHORD

With the six-four chord, something absolutely new happens. The six-four chord is a chord that opens doors. It's a chord that announces the cadenzas in concertos. It's a chord that leaves tonal space for something to happen. As you know, it is an extremely important chord in the cadence *[playing and naming the chords]*, the one (six-four) . . . five-seven . . . one:

EXAMPLE 7-8. The six-four chord in a cadence.

. . . . If every event in life could be as completely satisfactory as that! That just says all that needs to be said.

In the Brahms *B-Flat Concerto*, after the beautiful horn opening *[playing the horn solo on the piano]*:

EXAMPLE 7-9. Brahms, *Piano Concerto in B-flat Major*, op. 83, opening.

. . . the piano enters. . . . The piano has stopped *[third measure]* on a six-four chord. You feel a marvelous combination of rest and expectation, of poise leading onward to more movement. And of course *[playing the horn solo in measures four and five]* . . . the movement comes.

If you look at Chopin and Schumann you will find these beautiful combinations of sixth chords and six-four chords—these absolutely inevitable progressions of tones. This wonderful mazurka begins with an inverted *[diminished]* seventh (1):

EXAMPLE 7-10a. Chopin, *Mazurka,* op. 17, no. 4, opening.

. . . *[playing and naming chords]* sixth chord (2) . . . six-four chord (3), sixth chord (4) . . . six-four chord (5) . . . and we stop on the sixth (6). . . . Then we begin with the six-four (7) . . . sixth chord (8) . . . sixth chord (9) . . . sixth chord (10) . . . sixth chord (11) . . . *[continuing to play]*. . . . All the time we're floating in this wonderful meditative music . . . always these sixth chords. . . . Seven, six (12) . . . seven, six (13) . . . and at last, for the first time . . . five–one (14) . . . after all that time, all that beautiful holding of tone.

And this is what we can do with children. We can hold the tone, we can hold the sound, we can hold the dynamic forces—without end—until the moment comes for the five–one, for the affirmation of the chords in the root position, and of the great relationship of the dominant to the tonic.

Sybil: Which one is that you were playing?
Paul: That is number thirteen, and it's one of the most exquisite things that's ever been written. The very end of the composition is exactly as it began:

EXAMPLE 7-10b. Chopin, *Mazurka*, op. 17, no. 4, ending.

The melody . . . descends to the tonic (15). . . . There is the same progression of chords, and the piece ends on a sixth chord (16), that's it.

Alfred: Very modern idea.
Paul: Schumann's written one that ends on a six-four chord.

May I play you something else? What would this composition be without the sixth chord?

EXAMPLE 7-11. Chopin, *Etude,* op. 25, no. 9, opening.

. . . . With every second beat there comes the sixth chord, *[singing]* . . . tum, aahh! tum, aahh! *[gesturing to indicate movement from contracting to expanding, from closing to opening]*— you could do such beautiful movements to this. This is another idea you can take in working for a child. A chord in the root position . . . perhaps a seventh chord, any chord—and then a chord in inversion:

EXAMPLE 7-12. Improvisation, alternating a chord in root position with inversions and other chords.

. . . wonderful experiences you're giving a child, tonally and harmonically.

Here's a very simple prelude that you all know so well, but I wonder if you've ever realized what goes on in it:

continued on next page

continued from preceding page

EXAMPLE 7-13. Chopin, *Prelude*, op. 28, no. 20, opening.

. . . *[pausing after the first four measures]*. . . . Every chord is in the root position,[2] and only now *[continuing]* . . . ah! that first sixth chord (17), it's just the sun coming out of the clouds. It's a new being coming into this piece of music. . . . Another one (18) . . . and sevenths (19, 20) . . . and so on. It's the way he combines sixth chords and seventh chords—two of which are also not in root position—that gives this part of the music its elevated quality. And then it descends into the firmness and gravity of the chords in root position again, which are there on every beat of the closing measure.

I think this is what one must know about music. This is what one must meditate about music. And this is what must come into one's therapy.

There's something else I want to show you. This is Schumann again, this is from the *Carnaval*, and again, we begin on the sixth chord:

[2] Treating the third chord, measure one, as a suspension into the five-seven chord.

EXAMPLE 7-14. Schumann, "Eusebius," from *Carnaval*, op. 9, first section.

. . . and on this sixth chord he does *[playing the first measure and stopping on the first chord of the second measure]*. . . . Oh, isn't it just heaven! *[Beginning the piece again and playing the first four-measure phrase]*. . . . And the phrase ends with a six-four chord. *[playing the next four measures and continuing into the third phrase]*. . . . Sixth (21) . . . altered (22) . . . *[repeating (21) and (22)]* first this sixth . . . then this sixth . . . *[continuing]* six-four (23). . . . And that dominant seventh is so beautiful there (24). *[plays the fourth four-measure phrase]*. . . . That's how that ends. Now that's a wonderful rhythm, isn't it? Seven, and two against seven; four against seven; three against seven.

When you work with the six-four chords, be aware of this:

EXAMPLE 7-15. Improvisation, six-four chords with melodies in octaves above them.

. . . play a six-four chord (25), then first play notes contained in the chord in octaves above it, or sing them. . . . Include nonchordal tones as you continue. . . . Then go to a sixth chord (26) . . . and do the same thing.

And Ravel has written a very beautiful song—it's one of the three songs of Don Quixote to Dulcinea—it's called *Epic Song*, and starts entirely with six-four chords:

EXAMPLE 7-16. Ravel, *Chanson Epique* from *Don Quichotte à Dulcinée*.

. . . marvelous, marvelous sound.

You must have these in your fingers and be able to use them. Don't think "I've played seven of them and that's too many, I should now do a different one." When you're working with a child, there is timelessness. Time-less-ness. From the moment you begin your music and the child begins his activity, time ceases to exist. You create a *tonal time* with the dynamics of tone and all of its forces, all of its beauty. You and the child can live in this time. I felt that at the piano, Andrew *[a child in therapy]* and Knud were living in this—just what I'm talking about—this kind of time that has nothing to do with "It's now nearly five of three and I'm very tired," nothing to do with that. It's a completely different time. It's experiential time. It's the time in which you and the child are together in a musical experience. And if you play 569 six-four chords and sixth chords it doesn't matter one bit, as long as the life is there, the child is there, you are there. Nothing drops, everything keeps in the beautiful, magical timelessness in which real therapy takes place.

So all of music begins to look absolutely new through what therapy has made one realize about it. If it's become new for me, and can become new for you, and we can finish this course with the feeling that we have been on a great musical adventure—we have learned to use music in a new way, we have seen children respond and change—I think we'll all say we've had a very rich experience.

EXPLORATION EIGHT
TRIADS AND INVERSIONS IN THEIR RELATION TO THE INTERVAL CONCEPT

*R*elating the feeling for tonal directions, and the insight gained from the interval concept, to triads: in root position, in inversions, and with roots doubled. The triad as an event, as a musical statement. Combining intervals to form major and minor triads, sixth, and six-four chords. How intervals combine their experiential dynamics differently and so imbue chords with distinctive expressive qualities. Using the triad with freedom from conventional harmonic training. Exploring the elevation of the sixth chord and the expectancy of the six-four chord. Tonal directions creating harmonic movement. Debussy's free use of chords as an inspiring model for clinical musicianship in improvisational music therapy.

Let's just cast our minds back a bit to the things we have covered. We have talked about tonal directions. First of all, that each tone has a force, that each tone has directions—these are tones within the scale system, of course—and these tones have their relationships. They want to go *[pointing out on the blackboard]* here, here, here, and here. We take them where they want to go, if it's suitable in the music—or we make what we came to call a creative leap, and take the tone in a direction it doesn't naturally want to go, and we work from there. You remember that. You also remember the concept of the intervals, which was early in the first semester, and which has proven to be so important, I think. All along we've been able to refer to this concept of the intervals.

THE INTERVALLIC COMPONENTS OF TRIADS AND INVERSIONS

Now when we have a triad—a C . . . and an E . . . and a G . . . *[starting on middle C, playing the tones in succession and holding them]*—we have what intervals?

Students: Major third and minor third.
Paul: And what else?
Students: A fifth.
Paul: A major third, a minor third, and a perfect fifth *[playing and holding the triad . . . then playing it again, adding the C above middle C to play C–E–G–C . . . and holding the triad].* . . . Nothing's happened. Nothing is going to happen until I move somewhere else.

But *[playing C–E–G]* . . . to sink yourself deeply into this experience, or *[playing the C minor triad C–E♭–G]* . . . this experience, in which the thirds change places—and instead of major–minor we have minor–major *[C–E♭–G]* . . . this can be a very calming, soothing, relaxing experience. . . . The trick is that you mustn't think of anything else. You must just listen *[repeats and holds C–E♭–G].* . . .

But the moment I do this *[the F minor triad C–F–A♭]* . . . and take this *[C–E♭–G]* . . . to this *[C–F–A♭]* . . . expectations are aroused. Now what is going to happen? There is a future here. There's the possibility for music. It doesn't want to stop there. It wants to go on *[playing the B-flat major triad D–F–B♭]* . . . somewhere *[F–B♭–D]* . . . ; it wants to move.

Now, it's so fascinating that *[C–E♭–G]* . . . when you double the root *[C–E♭–G–C]* . . . everything changes. Why do you suppose that is? *[repeats C–E♭–G–C]*. . . . Let's go back to the triad again *[C–E♭–G]*. . . . Let's connect the triad to the concept we have of the intervals. The interval of the third was an inner experience in which there was balance within us, a balance within our inner self—our inner emotional self, our inner thinking self. There is a balance in this third *[C–E♭]* . . . which tends a little bit in one direction, and this major third *[E♭–G]* . . . which tends in another direction. In the triad we have these two balanced intervals *[C–E♭–G]* . . . plus the fifth interval, which you will remember is the interval *[C–G]* . . . in which we are facing the outside world. We haven't taken a step toward it yet, have we? We're just waiting there *[C–E♭–G]*. . . . So we're waiting in a state of balance, the wonderful thing about the triad.

FREEING TRIADS FROM HARMONIC TRADITION

One has to divorce the triad from one's conventional harmonic training, and begin to think of the triad as something one can use quite freely in therapy in quite a different way, without the harmonic connections you've been told and taught. This is an event *[C–E♭–G]* . . . ! This is an occurrence *[F–A–C]* . . . ! This is a challenge *[A♭–C–E♭]* . . . ! And yet *[D♭–F♭–A♭]* . . . every one of them is just absolutely balanced and controlled *[G–B–D]*. . . . Do this *[B♭–D♭–F]* . . . for a child *[D–F♯–A . . . then F–A♭–C]*. . . . Marvelous experiences with just the triad, the little old boring triad *[C–E♭–G]*. . . .

There's a wonderful piece of Debussy's that starts:

EXAMPLE 8-1. Debussy, *Prelude*, Book 2, no. 6, "General Lavine-eccentric," opening.

. . . [playing through the ninth measure]. . . . They're all root position triads—it's so charming and delightful—and absolutely freed from traditional harmony, used for what each one is in itself: An event! An experience!

Now, you double the root *[C–E♭–G–C]. . . .* What intervals do you add?

Students: The fourth, sixth, octave.

Paul: You add the perfect fourth, you add the sixth *[E♭–C] . . .* and you add the octave *[C–C]. . . .* Now in the octave *[C–C] . . .* you remember, was the experience of finding oneself in balance in the outer world. The sixth was the first step out one took from the fifth *[E♭–C]. . . .* The fourth was the movement from the third to the fifth. All of these things now combine *[C–E♭–G–C] . . .* the moment you simply double the fundamental tone of the triad.

Now, listen! Here is such a beautiful example of this—what composers instinctively feel! This is Debussy. You will hear a good bit of Debussy today and tomorrow, because he was primarily the one who freed chords from the relationships of the traditional harmony of the past. He more than anyone. Debussy is still not properly understood. Listen to what he does with triads with doubled roots:

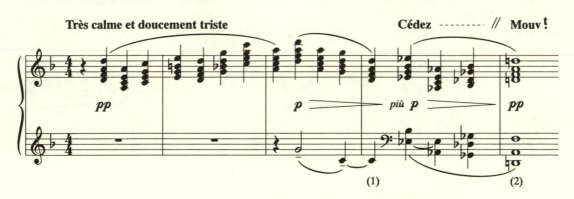

EXAMPLE 8-2a. Debussy, *Prelude,* Book 2, no. 10, "Canope," opening.

[Playing through (1)]. . . . Now with tripled roots *[continuing to (2)]. . . .* Isn't that beautiful . . . !

Alfred: It's one of my favorites.
Paul: Named after a star, "Canope," in French.
Clive: Canopus.
Alfred: You know, it always makes me think of something very primeval.
Paul: It makes me think of looking at a star: the wonderful distance of that star; the absolute steadfastness of it; its absolute security in the heavens. You could paint yourself marvelous pictures.

At the very end, Debussy doubles these chords:

EXAMPLE 8-2b. Debussy, *Prelude,* Book 2, no. 10, "Canope," approaching the conclusion.

. . . *[playing the concluding measures of the piece]* so that you have them in both hands. . . .
He uses a different harmony now (3). . . .

This is a superb example. Now just think of using chords like that: you've got a delicate child, not a very active child, you want to create a mood. Come here, Jane, do a little quiet, half-frightened drum beating. You're a shy little girl. We've just met, we're seeing each other for the first time. I've given you the brushes, and you're going to begin:

EXAMPLE 8-3. Clinical improvisation: triads in the style of the preceding example.

. . . . Thank you, Jane, that was lovely, and a lovely response.

Jane W.: It was lovely, thank you.
Paul: You enjoyed that?
Jane W.: Yes, I did.
Paul: You see what a wonderful mood you can create with just this beautiful
          thing which, as I say, we take so much for granted. And you see how
          important it is that clinical improvisation is absolutely without any but
          the most tenuous relationship to traditional harmonic instruction.

THE SIXTH CHORD

Now let's go back again to this beautiful, still not completely understood triad *[C–E–G]*. . . .
We're going to invert it. You all know what I mean by inverting? We're going to do that
[E–G–C]. . . . Instead of having a chord *[C–E–G]* . . . that is balanced with two thirds and a
fifth, what do we have now *[E–G–C]* . . . ? Three, four, six, don't we? We have—fascinating
to think of this—we have the three, we have the interval that's moving away from the
three, and we have the interval that's gone beyond the five. So the moment one has a sixth
chord *[E–G–C]* . . . one has a completely different experience. The first inversion of the
triad *[E–G–C]* . . . is not just a device, it's not something that has evolved. It is also an event
[E–G–C] . . . , a very important event. You remember:

EXAMPLE 8-4. Beethoven, *Piano Sonata in C Major*, op. 2, no. 3, third movement, opening.

. . . that marvelous Beethoven sonata. You remember how beautiful it is *[repeating the first two measures slowly]* . . . to hear those in sequence. It's absolutely thrilling, because what you're getting is a repetition of the same experience all the time, fluttering before your ears. Wonderful experiences: three–four–six! You're not outside yourself. You haven't found yourself yet in the octave. You haven't had the tension experience of the seventh. But you're on your way, and yet there's such control in it.

THE SIX-FOUR CHORD

[Returning to the initial triad, C–E–G]. . . . So, having meditated deeply on this, and feeling better men and women as a result, we have played the first inversion *[E–G–C]* . . . and experienced *[repeating E–G–C]* . . . the beautiful *[E–G–C]* . . . intervals *[E–G–C]* . . . of the fourth and the sixth, with the balance of the third held. Now we're going to invert it a second time *[G–C–E]*. . . . We have the same intervals, but in a different relationship. The fourth is below instead of above, and what a tremendous difference that makes. *[playing E–G–C, and then the first two measures of the Beethoven sonata, Example 8-4]*. . . . If I did:

EXAMPLE 8-5. Beethoven, *Piano Sonata in C Major,* op. 2, no. 3, right hand, substituting six-four chords for sixth chords.

. . . how different the experience would be. It isn't the same thing at all. *[G–C–E]* . . . I think we mentioned at the end of the second term *[G–C–E]* . . . what a beautiful feeling one has with the six-four chord that something must happen. And it does in the concerto, where you have:

EXAMPLE 8-6. Improvisation, entering into a cadenza through a six-four chord.

. . . . The orchestra stops, the pianist takes a deep breath and hopes to God he won't make a mistake, and embarks on his cadenza. What other chord could announce the cadenza but the six-four chord? If I did:

EXAMPLE 8-7. Improvisation, entering into a cadenza through a sixth chord.

. . . . *[the students laugh]*, it's comical, isn't it? It really is funny. But these are things we don't think about, we take them so for granted. So to use six-four chords with a child, you're just opening the door all the time for that child. You're raising curtains all the time for that child.

In Debussy again, this wonderful example in one of his better-known and (one could almost say) more hackneyed pieces, you come to the climax of this:

EXAMPLE 8-8. Debussy, *Prelude*, Book 1, no. 10, "La Cathédrale Engloutie" (The Sunken Cathedral).

. . . . Every one's a six-four chord *[(4) onward, referring to the chord forms themselves, disregarding the bass C pedal point]*, every one. And it has this tremendous nobility that the six-four chord has.

I can show you another example of the power of the six-four chord through the kindness of a friend who sent me the first page of *Salome*. The opera has no overture. The curtain goes up to an ascending scale on a clarinet:

EXAMPLE 8-9. Richard Strauss, *Salome*, opening.

. . . and you are right away on a six-four chord (5) . . . *[played by woodwinds, muted trumpets, and tremolo strings]* that awakens the mood of expectation right at the very beginning of the opera, just for one measure. The clarinet ascends further as an introduction, the Captain of the Guard *[Narraboth]* sings: "Wie schön ist die Prinzessin Salome heute nacht!" ("How fair is the Princess Salome tonight!") And we're off.

   You will find examples over and over again of the composers' sensitivity to this particular chord. And as you know, it's enormously important in the cadence:

. . . *[playing the cadence . . . then repeating, naming the chords]* one . . . six-four . . . five-seven . . . one. . . . All right? Forget it! *[laughter from the students]* We're not going to use it like that. Except when we want to. Except when it's right to. But we must also be able to use these chords quite freely and with clinical directness.

BALANCING TONAL DIRECTIONS AND RHYTHMIC FREEDOM

Let's just take a breather and look at what another composer has done with the sixth chord and the six-four chord. This time it's Schumann, and this is from the *Carnaval*. We looked at it briefly last time but there is so much originality in this piece, so much of creative interest, that I think we should look at it more closely. The rhythmic structure should be interesting to you because it's in 2/4 time, but the melody in the right hand is seven. The left hand plays two against seven. Then it changes to five on the first beat and three on the second beat. Then you have to play three against the five and the two. So there's a wonderful, creative rhythmic freedom Schumann has, but first, let's just listen to the chords.

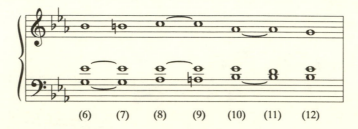

EXAMPLE 8-10a. Schumann, *Eusebius* from *Carnaval*, op. 9, harmonic progression, first phrase.

[Leading the students through the tonal directions and resulting chords] He starts first with the sixth chord (6). . . . He then raises the B♭ to B♮ (7). . . . This immediately has a direction *[holding (7)]*. . . ; where does it want to go? *[Student sings C.]* . . . Up! Exactly (8). . . . So up it goes—we've got a triad now *[repeating (8)]*. . . . He does the same thing with the lower note *[repeating (8) . . . then playing (9)]*. . . . What does that want to do? *[Students sing B♭.]* . . . It wants to rise, doesn't it? *[playing (7) to (8)]*. . . . They're so beautiful, these tonal directions (10). And then, the dominant seventh (11) resolves to the six-four chord (12). . . . So we start with a sixth chord, and the phrase ends with a six-four chord. And with the melody it's:

EXAMPLE 8-10b. Schumann, *Eusebius* from *Carnaval*, op. 9, first phrase, first eight measures.

[Playing first four measures]. . . . Perfection, isn't it? . . . [playing the second phrase, measures five through eight, then leading the students through the tonal directions and chords in the third phrase]:

(13)   (14)   (15)   (16)   (17)   (18)   (19)   (20)   (21)   (22)

EXAMPLE 8-10c. Schumann, *Eusebius* from *Carnaval*, op. 9, harmonic progression, third phrase.

Now the middle part starts with a sixth chord again (13) . . . the D in the left hand moves down to D♭ (14). . . . What does that want to do? *[Students sing the direction.]* . . . It wants to go down. The others wanted to go up, this one wants to go down, to C (15) . . . then down to B♮ (16). . . . He brings it back (17) . . . the tone that has changed can always come back to its starting point. . . . So we go *[recapitulating from (13)].* . . . We rest for a moment on the triad (18) . . . and then a sixth chord (19) . . . another sixth chord (20) . . . the sixth chord is changed (21) . . . and it goes to the dominant seventh (22) . . . and we're back to the first phrase. . . .

EXAMPLE 8-10d. Schumann, *Eusebius* from *Carnaval*, op. 9, third phrase, leading into fourth phrase.

[Recommencing playing at the ninth measure] Now, rhythmically, the middle part has the five (13), three (14), and so forth *[plays to the end of the example]*. . . .

So the whole thing—it doesn't have the triad in the root position at all *[except for those already named]*. The whole thing is up on a kind of a floating musical experience in which this rhythm plays its marvelous role in the melody. I think it's one of the loveliest things he ever wrote. You don't get the triad firmly in the root position until the repetition, in the twenty-fourth measure, finally. But it doesn't end that way. The very end comes, again, on a six-four chord.

So when you bring children experiences of the six-four chord:

. . . you're bringing them wonderful experiences of nobility, of opening, of possibility.

May I show you something else? You know, I just love to share these things with you because they excite me so—what composers *do* with *music!* Here is a composition of Debussy in three sharps, so it's in A major, it's in a major key:

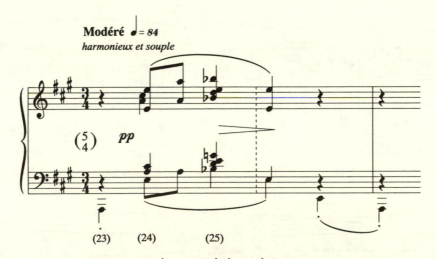

EXAMPLE 8-11. Debussy, *Prelude*, Book 1, no. 4, opening.

He plays the A (23) . . . so much music begins with a single tone. You remember, we've mentioned that before. He plays the A *[repeating it]* . . . immediately plays the A–C♯–E . . . but as a six-four chord (24) . . . *[begins the measure again]* . . . and does that *[the progression (23)–(24)–(25)]*. . . . That tremendous unexpected chord (25)—the moment you hear it—is absolutely right. This is genius, isn't it?

You will find, when you study the works of Debussy, that there is a basic musical structure he seldom abandons, and that is the relationship of five and one. No matter how free the harmony, no matter how dissonant it might seem, you will find the relationship of the dominant and the tonic is there, and it gives its underpinning. Look at this:

EXAMPLE 8-12. Debussy, *Prelude*, Book 2, no. 3, *La Puerta del Vino*, opening.

. . . . Wonderful! (26) D-flat major . . . *[repeating measures three and four]* . . . you could do it for hours. And what happens? *[Plays (27)–(28), and holds the Db, Ab, F, and B].* . . . What is that? It's *a dominant seventh chord!* A dominant seventh chord that never resolves. This is what I mean by Debussy freeing chords from their traditional role in harmony and using them in an absolutely new way.

    [Recommencing the piece at measure three]. . . . Now what . . . ? *[playing into measure nineteen].* . . . D-flat major at last (29)! Glorious, isn't it?

Amanda: What's it called?
Paul: *La Puerta del Vino,* "The Door of the Vineyard." It's a marvelous one!

I must show you this third and fourth measure of the same wonderful prelude that starts with the six-four chord:

EXAMPLE 8-13. Debussy, *Prelude,* Book 1, no. 4, "Les Sons et les Parfums Tournent dans l'Air du Soir"
(The Sounds and Fragrances Waft in the Evening Air).

. . . five–one *[E–A in the bass]* (30) . . . six-four chord (31). . . . Ta-tum (32), remember that: ta-tum-tum *[singing F#–C#–C#].* . . . And these *[chords in the left hand, (33) onward]* . . . are all dominant seventh chords, every single one.

DEBUSSY'S CONTRIBUTION TO CREATIVE FREEDOM

It's from this kind of freedom that a real music therapy—a clinical improvisational therapy—could come into being. Because if this hadn't taken place, we just wouldn't be here today. This has paved the way musically for all the things we now do, for our deliberate, conscious use of each harmonic element, each musical component. We owe Debussy a tremendous amount, as therapists, just for this very reason.

Wonderful creative freedom. This is what we must have in therapy—creative freedom— but tailored to the child, suited to the child, challenging the child, stimulating, arousing, supporting. We must have this beautiful creative freedom. And it's nothing that's given. You have to work for it. You won't be able to do more than you are able to do. You won't be able to bring more to the child than you have in your heart, in your mind, in your fingers, in your whole body as a *living music* with which to transmit the experiences the child must have.

EXPLORATION NINE
TWO MUSICAL EVENTS

The effect of the change of a single tone in a melody. The effect of a change of chord in a harmonic structure. A singing exercise exploring different harmonizations of a single tone. The harmonic-emotional experience of inversions. A playing exercise illustrating different harmonizations of a melodic idea, using essentially root position triads and first and second inversions.

There are two musical events that I think you would do well to continually sharpen your perception and awareness of. One event is the difference a tone can make in a melodic phrase or in a harmonic sequence—the change of one tone. This is a tonal event, and it's something that we must become very aware of, very sensitive to in our work. The other event is what a change of harmony can do. So we have on the one hand the single tone, and on the other the single harmony, which when changed at the right psychological moment can have a tremendous effect.

AN EXPRESSIVE CHANGE OF TONE IN A MELODY

As an example of the change of a single tone, may I just play you the first phrases of a piece from Schumann's *Davidsbündler:*

EXAMPLE 9-1. Schumann, *Davidsbündler,* op. 6, no. 5, opening.

. . . *[playing the first four-measure phrase].* . . . How many of you know that? Isn't it beautiful? *[repeating the phrase].* . . . Can you remember it? I'll play it one more time. . . . Now listen to the second phrase *[completes the example].* . . . One note (1) changed in that melody and we're just lifted into a completely different experience—and it happens at just the right time. If *[recommencing the example]* . . . Schumann had done *[placing the B at (2)]* . . . it wouldn't be the same thing at all. But the fact is *[beginning again]* . . . that he chose the one skip . . . that minor third (3), and made it into . . . a fifth (1) in the second phrase.

[The effect of the change is enhanced beautifully by the changes of the melodic tones that immediately follow the skips: after the minor third (3) the melody descends in steps, but after the fifth (1), the melody descends in skips along the tones of an E-minor triad. The melodic dynamics of the two phrases relate well to the schema of inherent tonal directions developed in Explorations Two and Three. The skip from the second tone of the scale to the fourth tone (3) follows a natural direction, whereas the skip from the second scale tone to the sixth tone (1) has the character of a creative leap, which is very distinct in this example. The descending tones following both the skip and the creative leap follow the inherent directions of tones.]

The change of one tone in your singing phrases to the children—in your goodbye songs, your hello songs—can do so much. But that one tone must be the right tone to change: the right tone in the phrase; the right tone within the musical context of the entire piece.

AN UPLIFTING CHANGE OF HARMONY

Now as an example of what a change of harmony can do, I will again play a composition of Schumann's, also from the *Davidsbündler*. And this is a wonderfully complicated—rhythmically complicated—piece. It's in 3/4 time: one, two, three, one, two, three. Part of it is divided *[as if in 6/8]* into *one*-two, *three*-four, *five*-six; the other is *one*-two-three, *four*-five-six. So you have two triplets in the measure as well as the underlying one, two, three—a beautiful thing to have done, musically. But the point is what he does with the idea harmonically. Again, you have this wonderful daring of Schumann:

continued on next page

continued from preceding page

EXAMPLE 9-2. Schumann, *Davidsbündler*, op. 6, no. 2, opening.

. . . *[commencing the piece and pausing after the first measure]*. . . . You don't know what key you're in, you have no idea. You're just immediately plunged into a mood *[recommencing the piece, playing the first section through the first ending; repeating and playing through the second ending]*. . . . There it is! (4), *[playing through into the second measure of the second section]*. . . . Nothing has changed: the rhythm is the same, the whole melodic structure is the same—instead of a half-step, D–C♯ (5)–(6) . . . we now have a whole step, G♯–F♯ (4)–(7) . . . which already makes all the melodic difference that's necessary. And you get that absolutely uplifting, refreshing, moving change of the harmony, not only because it's in a higher register—he could have done anything in the higher register—but because it is what it is, and it begins the second section of this wonderful composition—a small masterpiece.

And so with those two things in mind, I have composed a little exercise with which I think we might have some harmonic experiences together.

HARMONIZATIONS WITH A COMMON SUNG TONE

EXAMPLE 9-3. Singing exercise for harmonic experience.

[Playing the three-measure phrase, (8)–(10)]. . . . We'll sing each tone on "la." All right, we'll sing it together. *[The students sing the phrase.]* . . . Good!

Nancy, sing it to a child standing here, and *[singing to exemplify]* . . . give it all your voice! *[Nancy sings the phrase; as she holds the ending tone A, chord (10) is played.]* . . . That was good!

Knud! *[As Knud concludes the phrase, chord (11) is played.]* . . . This is experience, isn't it!

Tom! *[Chord (12) is played as Tom concludes the phrase.]* . . . All right.

Jane! *[As each student in turn sings the phrase, a different harmony is put to the final A. The students are surprised and excited by the contrasting results.]* . . .

If we took the time to list the harmonic possibilities on that one note A, you would just be astonished. There must be dozens. So that if you are improvising:

EXAMPLE 9-4. Improvisation ending with harmonizations of the tone A.

. . . you have so many possibilities that will arouse the child, bring him back into consciousness, focus him again. So that you don't always stay in the same tonality; you don't always feel constrained. You've got these possibilities, but you've got to work on them. You've got to get them into your fingers.

THE HARMONIC-EMOTIONAL EXPERIENCE OF INVERSIONS

I've been accompanying your singing with sixth chords *[playing the progression (8)–(9) slowly, emphasizing the chords]*. . . . Now listen to it with six-four chords:

. . . quite a different thing! Now I'll play one, then the other. The sixth . . . *[alternating the sixth chord and six-four chord variations for contrast]*. . . . The second inversion already makes a tremendous change, as we saw last week.

   [The session is recessed and resumed later. A second melody is introduced, and the effects of alternative harmonies and different chord forms are explored.]

EXAMPLE 9-5. Lyric melody with alternative harmonizations.

There are two ways in which this melody could be harmonized, and I'll play them one after the other, so you hear how very different they are.

. . . [playing harmonization (a) with chords in root position, and then harmonization (b) with chords in first inversion]. . . . Which of the two do you think has more life, more character?

Students: The second one.

Paul: The second one. It's wonderful what the inversion does. It supports the melody in a completely different way.

Nancy: Paul, do you think there's a place for the first one—that that's a different mood?

Paul: Why, certainly. Of course.

Nancy: But the other one is much stronger.

Paul: But this [harmonization (b)] does what we said it does: it has more life in it, it has more movement in it, it supports the melody more. This [harmonization (a)] is something that's more stable, it's calmer, it's less demanding, it moves at a much slower pace. Even though the tempo is the same, the actual movement of harmonic experience is constant, and has the constancy of the triad in the root position.

Now this is going to be a little mixture. Jane, would you play this for us?

[referring to harmonization (c)] We begin with the triad on A (13), not an inversion. We have a sixth chord here (14), a sixth chord here (15), and a six-four chord to cover the two beats (16). Do you want to play the melody first?

  [Jane plays the melody.] . . . Good. Begin with the triad, that's right, use that position, A minor. *[Jane plays (13).]* . . . It's a completely different thing, isn't it? *[continuing the example, playing the second chord of measure two on the fourth beat].* . . . Good! Starting out of the key—starting away from the idea of its tonal focus of C major—we already give the melody a completely different emotional experience. Play this one; compare them *[indicating the first phrase of (a), the first phrase of (b), and then (c) in its entirety].* . . . Thank you very much! So there again, we have a different experience when we start out of the key—*[repeats harmonizations (a), (b), and (c) in their entirety].* . . . As Dr. Marshack *[the psychology instructor to the course]* would say, "We have so many options." Our music needn't be dull for the children.

  [Jean is asked to come to the piano.] Again we're going to start with the triad in the root position (17)—you can take the top note with your right hand, if you like—then a sixth chord (18), a six-four chord (19), and then two triads in root position (20) and (21). Do you want to play the melody first? I'm not tired of it yet, are you?

Students: No!

  [Jean plays the melody by itself, and then with the full harmonization. Jean works at the example.] . . . Good, play it again, you did it beautifully. *[The example is repeated.]* . . . Thank you very much, Jean!

  Now what I did here (17) was to sneak in a seventh chord, which we haven't come to yet. I couldn't resist it because of the wonderful difference that there is between this *[the first phrase of harmonization (c), with the A-minor triad in open root position (13)]* . . . and this *[the first phrase of harmonization (d), with the D-minor triad in open root position (17), supporting the C in the melody, producing the open voiced seventh chord D–A–F–C].* . . . The other progression *[repeating the beginning phrases of (c) and (d)]* . . . do you feel that F pulling down to the E *[chords (17) and (18)]* . . . ? Do you feel that direction that's living in F as a dynamic force? *[recommencing harmonization (d), playing through the first measure and arriving at (19)].* . . . There's the beautiful six-four that opens the window and lets the air in *[continuing to the end of the measure]* . . . , the relaxation of the two chords in the root position (20) and (21), and we've come to the dominant. . . . *[The example is completed by returning to the tonic, C major, in root position, as the opening triplet melodic figure is repeated.]* . . .

When you get a melodic idea, which some of you may begin to get—tunes which may begin to come into your head for your children to such words as "hello," "goodbye," "come beat the drum," "come play the piano"—remember the tune. Write it down, or play it over and over and over. Then find for it a harmony that is alive, a harmony that supports it, enhances it, moves it forward. And we'll begin to get some lovely, lovely harmonies in our improvisations for the children. And they have just the same effect on them as that wonderful harmonic change in the Schumann had on us. You can be sure of that.

EXPLORATION TEN
INVERSIONS AND THE DIRECTIONS OF TONES

*T*he importance of musical culture, and culture in general, as fields of enrichment and creative resources for music therapists. The great classical composers as explorers of the powers of expression in the tonal language of music. The free originality of Schumann as an example of creative intelligence. Suggestions for improvisation arising from Schumann's consistent use of a simple tonal movement. Using sixth, six-four, and seventh chords. Introducing the Catalonian composer Frederico Mompou, with particular reference to his use of sixth, six-four, and seventh chords.

Now let's have a little review going all the way back to the directions of a single tone, because I have such a beautiful musical example of this to show you today.

THE IMPORTANCE OF CULTURAL NOURISHMENT

In thinking about you, and in thinking about your future as music therapists, I am thinking about how absolutely necessary it is for you all to become musically cultured people. I could go even further and say how important it is that you become cultured people: that you know the great poems, the great novelists, the great painters. Because the more you feed into your own inner life, the richer that inner life is going to be—the more you're going to have to give from within that rich inner life to the children who come to meet you. That will all become part of you. If it's part of you, it's part of the musical you; if it's part of the musical you, it's part of the music you have to bring to a child.

Although it's interesting, naturally, to see what is happening today—to be contemporary, so to speak—and listen occasionally to concrete music, electronic music, synthesized music, atonal music, and all the rest, it's much more important for us as therapists really to get in our grasp the essentials of the greatness of the music of the past. Because these were the people—the Bach, the Mozart, the Beethoven, and so on—these were the people who worked with all of the things we need: with tremendous sensitivity to intervals; with an absolutely instinctive feeling for the directions of tone; who made the most beautiful creative leaps out of those tonal directions. These were the people who sensed the way chord progressions could be most expressive—most naturally, musically expressive.

BECOMING MORE AWARE OF TONAL DIRECTIONS

We'll come back to Beethoven in a moment, but just think: if I play this *[middle C#, sustained]* . . . at the moment it's meaningless. If I do *[C# then D]* . . . there is already a meaning in that first tone it did not have before, a significance it did not have before. *[C#]* . . . And now you are attentive *[D]* . . . your ear is aroused, you're waiting, what should happen? And when Schumann does:

EXAMPLE 10-1. Schumann, *Vogel als Prophet* (Bird as Prophet), op. 82, opening.

. . . (1)–(2)–(3). This is—you could weep over it—it's so absolutely perfectly beautiful. The C♯ (1) is taken to D . . . it's held, it's a dotted eighth—and then we have very quickly, skips along the G minor chord (2) . . . again to the C♯, and the G minor chord again (3) . . . *[playing through to (4)]. . . .* So wonderful . . . *[continuing to (5)].* The whole thing is based (1)–(2) . . .

on that direction of the tone to a tone a half-step above. *[playing a number of instances of melodic movements of an ascending half-step: D♯ to E over a sustained G–B♭ (6); G♯ to A in a D minor period (4); E to F in the context of an F major chord (7); in the left hand, F♯ to G in the context of C minor (8), and then in the context of G dominant seventh (9)].*

It's a piece well worth studying. Harmonically, it's free. It has beautiful silences: listen to them *[playing into the fifth measure and observing the completely silent rests in both hands after every phrase].* . . . . You don't know what's coming, and yet when it comes it's absolutely right, it's absolutely inevitable.

Clive: Paul, what is the name of it?
Paul: "Bird as Prophet," *Vogel als Prophet.*

MUSICAL LIMITS AS AIDS TO IMPROVISATION

Now in your work, in your improvisations at home, take a tone, take two tones. What can you do with them?

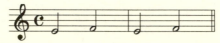

You can play them, of course, in all kinds of tempi with different rhythms:

You can play them as a trill:

You can play one as a ninth above the other, or you can split them into a seventh:

You can play them as octaves:

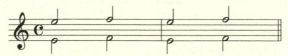

You can play the two intervals together:

You can build sixth chords on them,

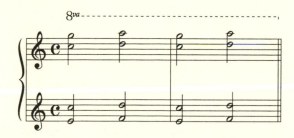

six-four chords,

or seventh chords:

I have a sneaking suspicion that the best practice for clinical improvisation is not free at all. The best practice is when you *limit* yourself to something, you give yourself a real limitation. *[The students agree.]* You've got organum chords . . . on those two notes, both forms:

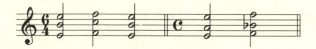

Why can't you have them in a pentatonic scale?

Students: You've got a semitone.
Paul: Because there is a semitone between them. There is no semitone in the
           pentatonic unless you deliberately alter the scale.

MOMPOU'S USE OF SIXTH, SIX-FOUR, AND SEVENTH CHORDS

In regard to the sixth chords, you're all familiar with them now. You all have used them, and you're practicing them every day until your fingers ache.

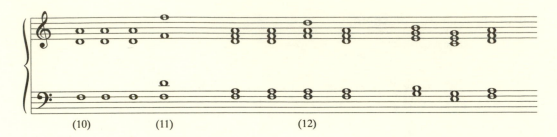

(10)   (11)   (12)

. . . The sixth chord (10) . . . we had different positions, we've discussed them (11). . . . We discussed the . . . big doublings that are possible (12) . . . and how beautiful they are.

I just ran across a remarkable composition by a very little-known composer, a Catalonian composer named Mompou who has written a great many deceptively simple compositions. I say they're deceptively simple because I think they have enormous importance. I think the man's creative gift is a very great one, and he himself is one of the most modest, one of the shyest, quietest persons you'd ever meet, with no idea at all that he's written important music.[1]

Now listen to what he does with sixth chords.

(13)

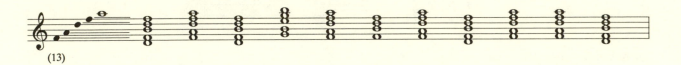

[Arpeggiating a sixth chord (13)]. . . . This is the sixth chord. [plays sixth chords underlying the harmonic structure of the treble voices in measures three through six of the following composition]. . . . Nice sound, isn't it? I don't think we have noted that particular position, but those of you who have been really . . . *[plays experimentally with the chord form]* . . . playing with them might have discovered them.

He begins this composition with a seventh chord (14), and he doubles the seventh so that you have:

(14)

---

[1] When Nordoff visited Mompou in Barcelona in the early 1950s, Mompou described himself as a "salon composer."

. . . marvelous sound. *[playing the opening two measures].* . . . Immediately we have an atmosphere, we have a mood:

EXAMPLE 10-2a. Mompou, *L'Ermita* from *Pressebres*, first section.

. . . *[continues reading through the first section].* Isn't that a beautiful use of sixth chords? *[repeats the section].* . . . Now he takes the doubled seventh idea (15) and does:

continued on next page

continued from preceding page

EXAMPLE 10-2b. Mompou, *L'Ermita* from *Pressebres*, second section.

. . . . Wonderful piece of music!

Sybil: What is that called, Paul?
Paul: It's called *The Hermitage,* and it's from a suite of pieces called *Pressebres*
           (Crèches). I think it is quite remarkable in almost all of his music how
           he uses the intervals.

Now, here again, in another composition by Mompou, we find the same idea that Schumann
used, but whereas Schumann used an ascending half-step, C#–D . . . in the Mompou we have
the half-step, E♭–D . . . descending (16). It happens with a B♭–E♭ . . . so you could think of
this G–B♭–E♭ (17) as either a sixth chord . . . or G–B♭–D as a chord in the root position. The
sixth chord comes on the first and the third of each four sixteenth notes.

(16) (17)

(18)

continued on next page

continued from preceding page

EXAMPLE 10-3a. Mompou, *Canción y Danza 2* (Song and Dance 2), song section.

This is the song. . . . Beautiful—doubling this third (18) of the chord two octaves higher.

EXAMPLE 10-3b. Mompou, *Canción y Danza 2* (Song and Dance 2), dance section.

This is the dance. . . . Tremendous charm!

Going back to this first part, the song, with these beautiful sixth chords—some of them become seventh chords as well—I think is well worth studying. And the wonderful subtle use of dissonance—when he does *[playing the phrase of Example 10-3a containing (19)]* . . . that E♮ *[repeating the tone]* . . . it's so marvelous, like a cry in the middle of the music! A wonderful bit of tension introduced.

Now, in thinking about six-four chords, take Mompou again and see what a lovely thing he does with six-four chords *[plays the beginning chords of the following composition, then moves the chord form freely in stepwise motion]* . . . the triad in the second inversion position; just absolutely straight:

EXAMPLE 10-4a. Mompou, *Fêtes Lointaines 5* (Far-Away Festivals 5), first section.

. . . seventh chord (20). . . . And still six-four:

continued on next page

continued from preceding page

EXAMPLE 10-4b. Mompou, *Fêtes Lointaines 5*, second section.

[Beginning the second section, illustrating the six-four chord configuration; with variations in the order of the measures]. . . . Six-four, and seven . . . [concludes the section]. . . .

I bring these examples in to you to give you some musical experience, and also to give you some idea of how absolutely wonderful these chords are, and the tremendous possibilities they have.

EXPLORATION ELEVEN
INTRODUCTION TO SEVENTH CHORDS

*T*he first step in freeing the seventh chords: liberating the dominant seventh from
its traditional function. The importance of the deceptive cadence. Beethoven's
frequent use of the deceptive cadence. The different forms of the seventh chord;
the study of their intervallic components as a key to understanding their emotional
impact. The power of the tritone. The diminished seventh chord; its multiple possibilities
for resolution. The liberating effect of inversions on the dominant seventh.

THE LIBERATION OF THE DOMINANT SEVENTH CHORD

Now the liberation of the seventh chords really began with the liberation of the dominant
seventh—and the person who took the first bold steps toward this was, can anyone tell me?

Student: Wagner?
Paul: No, that's later.
Jenny: The liberation of the dominant seventh?
Paul: Yes. How was it effected? What was the first step taken?
Amanda: That it wasn't resolved?
Jane W.: Wasn't there a suspension from the chord to the . . . ?"
Paul: Yes, but that's not really what I mean. Here we have it:

. . . . The first step taken to liberate this was when the dominant seventh was not taken to
the tonic, but taken to another harmony. And this, we were taught to call the deceptive
cadence. Were you taught that, too? Now, when Beethoven does:

EXAMPLE 11-1. Beethoven, *Piano Sonata in E-flat Major*, op. 81a, "Les Adieux," opening.

. . . (1) the dominant is implied there, isn't it, and does that (2) . . . it's not what you have expected at all *[plays to complete the opening statement]*. . . . Over and over again, you can find in Beethoven examples of the deceptive cadence—of the dominant going somewhere else than to its natural resolution, to the tonic. And this was the first freeing of the dominant from its function, its traditional function.

You must be aware of the fact that with three thirds—superimposed thirds—we're creating tonal worlds:

[The lowest B on the piano is sounded. . . . With the pedal held down, single B's are played freely in all registers, in a moderate tempo . . . the series of B's concludes with a sustained major seventh chord (3). . . . A second series of B's, similarly sustained with the pedal . . . concludes with a half-diminished seventh chord (4), also sustained. . . . The two chords are then played in succession for contrast.] . . .

They're fantastic in their emotional content, and this is certainly again another proof of the fact that in harmony, as in all the other parts of music—especially in harmony—we have a whole that is so much greater than the sum of its parts.

Because, we have in every seventh chord either stressed:

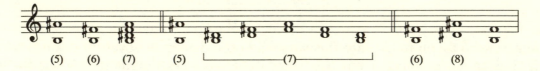

. . . in the major seventh we have this marvelous interval of tension (5). We also have this holding interval (6) . . . of the fifth, and we have three intervals (7) . . . of inner balance. So this chord contains, from our interval concept, a wonderful distribution—if I can use that word—of experience: the tension of the seventh (5) . . . the balance (7) . . . of the thirds . . . and the beautiful stability (6), (8) . . . of the fifths. . . .

Then, of course, we get different intervals when we change them.

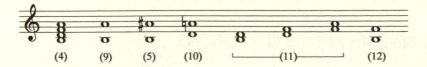

When we do this one (4) . . . the second one I played, we have a softer seventh (9) . . . it's not so full of tension as this (5). . . . It has more the gesture of a stretching . . . out than a trembling . . . , if I can say that. We have the fifth (10) . . . we have our thirds (11) . . . but we have as well (12) . . . this wonderful, mysterious interval of the tritone.

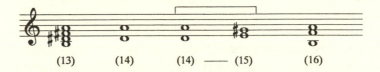

Now in the dominant seventh form (13) . . . with the major–minor–minor thirds, we also have the tritone (14) . . . and that tritone is the one that pulls it back (14)–(15) . . . to its tonic, through the directions, the tonal directions that we studied earlier. Isn't that fascinating?

Amanda: It's a real two-headed monster.
Paul: It's a two-headed monster! That's a very nice picture: (14) . . . one is pulling in and one is pulling out (15). . . .

And this is the result; without this tritone (14) . . . you wouldn't feel that demand. If I played the dominant seventh without the tritone (16) . . . it doesn't have at all what this has (13). . . . So that must be in the dominant seventh if it's to be real dominant seventh (14)–(15). . . .

Now let's look at one of the others:

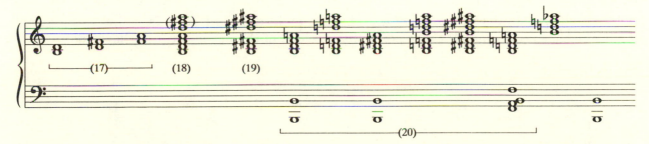

The minor–major–minor (17) . . . that's a beautiful one (18). *[playing a series of B's with the sustaining pedal held down . . . concluding with (18) . . . then alternating repetitions of B's with (18) . . . then with (19). . . . Plays a series of variously formed seventh chords, alternating and contrasting them in different registers (20 onward)].* . . .

I'd love you to do this. Play with seventh chords. All the things we do in here are supplementary to the exercises you have in *Creative Music Therapy*. All the work we do in here is meant to give you pleasure, it's meant to deepen your interest, deepen your perception, deepen your hearing, and also to give you some actual clinical practice that might be useful in therapy with children. You understand that.

Take a single tone and just have fun at home, build seventh chords, alternate them, combine them. Listen to each one intently, to the different character each one has.

THE DIMINISHED SEVENTH AND ITS RESOLUTIONS

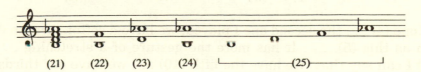

The diminished seventh, of course, has two tritones (21). . . . That's why it has this fantastic sound. It has this one (22) . . . and this one (23) . . . so it lacks the stability of the perfect fifth—it's not there. You're (22) . . . really *not* facing the outside world in a diminished chord (21). . . . There's a little sixth there (24) . . . which is a bit of a step. But you've got three minor thirds (25) . . . and you're living very intently within yourself (21) . . . in a condition of *tension*. . . . This wants to move, doesn't it? This doesn't want to stay where it is (21). . . . Where does it want to go?

[The students participate in experiencing the diminished seventh chord and in exploring its resolutions.] . . . You can take any one of the tones—this might be fun for you to do, too, I don't know if you ever did this in your courses of musical study—you can take any one of the tones of the diminished seventh and consider it a leading tone. Did you study those that way? So that with the diminished seventh on B (21):

> A♭, as G♯, can take you to A major or minor;
> B is the leading tone of C major or C minor;
> D is the leading tone of E-flat major or E-flat minor;
> F is the leading tone of G-flat major or G-flat minor, or
> (with the enharmonic change) of F-sharp major or F-sharp minor.

There is the possibility of resolving this chord to eight different keys, isn't that fascinating! That one chord contains all those possibilities. None of the other seventh chords do:

It's simply because of the wonderful tension in this chord (26) . . . *[then playing inversions of the chord]* (27) . . . I like it better when it's open . . . and moves. . . . Now we'll take the G♯ (A♭) as the leading tone (28) . . . *[resolving to A minor].* . . . *[continuing to play inversions of the diminished seventh on B . . . leading into resolutions to A major . . . C major . . . C minor . . . E-flat major . . . and E-flat minor].* . . . Marvelous! If we really could get all these things in our fingers, what we would have to use in our improvisations with the children. Simply wonderful!

THE DOMINANT SEVENTH AND ITS RESOLUTIONS

But with the dominant seventh:

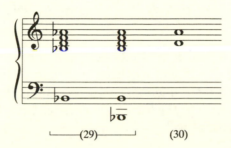

This one is on B♭ (29) . . . *[resolving to E-flat major].* . . . Now, there again (29) . . . because of this tritone (30) . . . you can take the D as the leading tone and resolve it to E-flat major . . . or to E-flat minor. . . .

Or you can take the A♭ . . . as the leading tone and take it up *[playing D major]* . . . or D minor . . . *[continuing with resolutions to A major . . . and A minor . . . and finally resolving again to E-flat major].* . . . Sounds very refreshing when you hear it in its original connection after taking it to all the chords that make it a deceptive cadence.

These are the things to play with, and to relax with after you have worked terribly hard on one of the exercises, and you want to have some fun—do a little slaving with seventh chords:

. . . it's liberated already from being a dominant seventh . . . the moment you begin to move up in the inversions (31) . . . *[resolving to G-flat major (32)].* . . .

EXPLORATION TWELVE
A SINGING EXPERIENCE WITH
SEVENTH CHORDS

*E*xperiencing a variety of seventh chords in relationship to a common sung tone. The impact of seventh chords in compositions by Mompou and Debussy. Seventh chords as components of melody. The message of "Pif-Paf-Poltrie."

Maybe we could have a drum and a cymbal—and a cymbalist and a drummerist. Put the cymbal over here—I can just direct you like that and like that, all right?

Now, you are going to begin the measure with no music, bang! *[tapping a single beat on the drum then singing the rhythm of the bass figure]* ta da tum, ta-tum . . . and we're all going to sing a tone. Is that clear, Annelise?

Annelise: *[at the drum and cymbal]* Very clear.
Paul: Good! I'm going to play this:

EXAMPLE 12-1a. An exercise in singing with seventh chords.

. . . . *[The bass figure is played . . . the class sings the C.]* . . . You can sing an octave higher if you like. *[The figure is repeated and the class sings octave C's.]* . . . Good! All right. Drum! [The exercise is played and sung.] . . . Hold it longer. Drum! [The exercise is repeated . . . with a further exhortation to hold the sung tone longer. . . . It is then repeated without interruption as, in successive repetitions, seventh chords (1) through (8) are played against the C; for the most part, each seventh chord is repeated twice as the C is held.] . . .

Aren't those lovely experiences? That cymbal should give you a little "frisson," as the French call it, a thrill.

Clive: Wouldn't it be better to play a tremolo on the cymbal, a softer tremolo
             before you play the chord, rather than a clout?

Paul: Let's try it:

EXAMPLE 12-1b. The exercise continues with changes in the bass figure and further examples of seventh chords.

. . . *[after the first repetition]* No! I want to hear the cymbal. . . . *[It is played firmly through
the remaining repetitions of the exercise; seventh chords (9) . . . (10) . . . (11) are played,
followed by augmented chord (12).]* . . .

    All chords possible with the one note C. Beautiful seventh chords with the one note C.
Knud! *[Knud strikes the drum to begin another repetition]:*

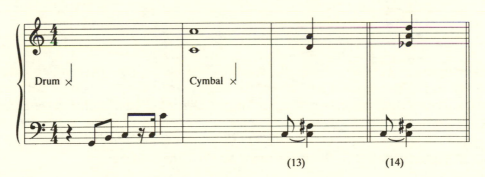

EXAMPLE 12-1c. The exercise continues with a further change in the bass figure and more examples of seventh chords.

. . . (13) and (14). . . . And so it goes.

    There are dozens of them; want some more? Isn't it fun?

    Play with your seventh chords, too, and appreciate the quality of every one. Change the
arrangement of the tones around so that the forms are different.

THE ROLES OF SEVENTH CHORDS

Do you remember that beautiful Mompou piece that started with the dominant seventh in
this position?

EXAMPLE 12-2. Mompou, *Prelude*, no. 10, opening.

(15) . . . just absolutely beautiful, isn't it? It's just riveting (15). . . . *[playing the chord down a half-step . . . then (15) again . . . playing an inversion of the chord . . . then briefly improvising in the style of the prelude].* . . . It's so original to do something like that with the dominant seventh chord.

And what Debussy does with dominant seventh chords in the wonderful "Soirée," that "Night in Grenada":

Mouvement de Habanera

Commencer lentement dans un rythme nonchalamment gracieux

EXAMPLE 12-3: Debussy, *La Soirée dans Granade* from *Estampes*, opening.

. . . which I shall never forget. *[playing through to measure twenty]*. . . . All dominant sevenths, every single one! *[repeating (16) to (17) slowly for emphasis]* . . . *[concluding the example with measure twenty-one (18)]*. . . .

THE SEVENTH CHORD IN MELODIC CONSTRUCTION

Isn't it breathtaking? It's so important, really, to free yourselves from all traditional tonal dependencies, harmonic dependencies, and to learn to use these chords absolutely with freedom—and to write a melody, construct a melody around the seventh chord. There is a perfectly good reason why this:

EXAMPLE 12-4a. Debussy, *Prelude*, Book 1, no. 8, "La Fille aux Cheveux de Lin," (The Girl with the Flaxen Hair), opening.

. . . *[playing the principal melodic statement]* . . . became such a popular piece: it's just absolutely beautiful! And what is it? Db'–Bb–Gb–Eb–Gb–Bb–Db' . . . it's the seventh chord made out of minor–major–minor *[the students join in identifying the intervals]* . . . and how absolutely beautiful it is . . . !

In the second part he takes the tones of the initial seventh chord and just plays with them like this:

EXAMPLE 12-4b. Debussy, *Prelude*, Book I, no. 8, "La Fille aux Cheveux de Lin," measures 24–32.

. . . *[playing in the style of the piece (19), moving the inverted seventh chord in open position up and down the keyboard].* . . . And then, I think something like this happens *[playing the C-flat major chord (20) and the original melody an octave higher]* . . . he puts it over a completely different harmony. . . . What a pretty girl she must have been . . . !

So make melodies with your seventh chords. They're not only for harmonies, they're for melodies:

EXAMPLE 12-5. Improvisation incorporating a dominant seventh chord.

. . . dominant seventh chords (21) . . . *[segueing to]:*

EXAMPLE 12-6. Nordoff and Robbins, *Sweeping Song, "Pif-Paf-Poltrie."*
Copyright 1961 and 1969 by Theodore Presser Co. Used with permission.

. . . . *[The students, familiar with the song from current group therapy practice with children, join in singing it. Note the use of seventh chords and inversions in this song.]*

Yes, that's the message of "Pif-Paf." Sweep it all clean! Sweep your music clean! Sweep yourselves clean! Sweep the children clean! Sweep the sessions clean! Okay, thank you very much.

EDITOR'S NOTE   Paul Nordoff's injunction to "Sweep it all clean" invites explanation. The reference is to the musical working game of "Pif-Paf-Poltrie," adapted from the Grimm's folk tale "Fair Katrinelje and Pif-Paf-Poltrie," which Nordoff and Robbins developed for variously disabled children at the very beginning of their collaboration.

The principal character in the tale, Pif-Paf-Poltrie, is a besom-binder (a besom is a folk term for a simple broom made of birch twigs or broom corn bound to a stick). The game starts with a mess of leaves and birch twigs or broom corn being spread on the floor. Pif-Paf-Poltrie's intention is to marry Fair Katie. To Pif-Paf-Poltrie's March he travels from one member of her family to another, gaining their consent. Fair Katie confirms her willingness with a gentle song. The class then sings and mimes working actions to a vigorous Working Song, as they ask Pif-Paf-Poltrie what he can do. The fulfillment of the game is realized as he proceeds to enact his response. To a Besom-Binding Song, the twigs or broom corn for a besom are gathered out of the mess of leaves and, with Pif-Paf's participation, bound to a stick to make the besom. Pif-Paf then takes on the challenge of sweeping the scattered leaves into a tidy central heap. As he sweeps, he is given as little or as much personal guidance as necessary, but most of his support comes from music improvised with his sweeping, and from a warm, serious Sweeping Song—the song the students sang to conclude Exploration Twelve. Pif-Paf-Poltrie's completion of his task is celebrated with a rhythmic song of affirmation. As the class sings And They All Lived Happily Ever After, the leaves are gathered into a basket, and the game comes to its conclusion.

In the context of the action of the game, the speech, and the music, the sweeping of the mess and the gathering up of the leaves assume much greater significance than that of a mere routine chore. The essential experience of the game, which the children live, combines making order out of disorder, "seeing something through," courage to face a challenge, and the exercising of purpose, concentration, attentiveness, goodwill, and responsibility. The children always enjoyed the game, and its results were seen in the development of awareness, confidence, self-esteem, a positive feeling of accomplishment, and a sense of well-being. It was in reference to these values that Exploration Twelve was brought to its closure.

EXPLORATION THIRTEEN
TENSION AND RELAXATION

*D*issonance and consonance as tension and relaxation; urgency in tonal directions. A historical examination of how composers have created, intensified, and extended tension throughout the development of Western music. Tension through melodic ornamentation and prepared nonchordal tones; through the superimposition of chords; through unprepared nonchordal tones. The building of tension through harmonic progressions; through silences; through dynamics. Tension that ebbs and flows through a composition. Tension through the loosening of tonality; through chromaticism; and through treating chords as independent expressive entities.

TECHNIQUES FOR CREATING MUSICAL TENSION

Let us stop thinking of dissonance and consonance, and begin to think in terms of tension and relaxation, of the increase in the urgency of tonal directions. You remember the urgency in the Schumann "Bird as Prophet" . . . the urgency of that C♯ (1). . . .

EXAMPLE 13-1. Schumann, *Vogel als Prophet,* op. 82, opening.

We must become sensitive to and look at the music we already know—and the music we are practicing and learning—if we are studying. The music you use in therapy must begin to have tension in its harmonic form, and both harmonically and melodically, a sense of urgency in the tonal direction—which immediately makes it necessary for movement to take place, for other tones to follow, just as it does in that simple example of the Schumann.

Now, there can be more or less tension, depending on the kinds of chords and the kinds of intervals you use. And there can be more—there can be less—relaxation, depending on the kinds of intervals and chords you use. An extreme example, of course:

EXAMPLE 13-2. Dominant-tonic resolution exercise from *Creative Music Therapy,* p. 227.

. . . is that. There can be more tension. If I were to do:

. . . *[modifying the dominant seventh chord by adding a minor second in the left hand, first beat]* . . . that's more tension than this *[playing the unmodified chord]*. . . . And if I did *[taking out the third of the tonic chord and adding the sixth at the third beat]* . . . that's a softer relaxation *[repeating the modified exercise]*. . . . It changes the whole character of the thing. It's not as simple a relaxation; it's not as complete a relaxation; but it's a softer relaxation.

Your degree of tension, your degree of relaxation, will depend entirely on the urgency of the forces that lie in the tones you use. A modern composer could take this idea of Schumann *[playing Example 13-1]* and do this:

. . . . This immediately increases the tension there. This would be a completely different effect. There would be much more tension, much less relaxation. So this will always depend, as I say and I will repeat it, on the degree of urgency, and the forces, the directional forces— *the desires*—the tones have that you are working with.

Melodic ornaments; prepared nonchordal tones

Now the need for tension and relaxation has been felt in music for hundreds of years. We won't go back any further than Rameau, but I like to quote this example because it has so many beautiful, instructive things in it:

EXAMPLE 13-3. Rameau, *Gavotte Variée* from *Pièces de Clavecin,* opening.

He begins—this is a gavotte with variations— . . . with a closed position of the A minor chord (2) . . . and just by taking two of those tones *[D and B]* . . . using them as passing tones, and going to higher tones in the same chord (3), he creates a melodic line *[playing the first two measures].* . . . Beautiful, isn't it?

[Repeating the second measure and continuing, playing with added embellishments] . . .

Six-four chord (4) . . . *[pausing after (6)]*. Now, what we had at that moment (5) was this *[on the blackboard, writing the chord at (5) as A–D–G♯]*. Just bear that in mind *[playing the chord as written and resolving it to A minor]* (6). . . . Very fleeting; it's immediately resolved, but we have a moment of tension there. May we hear it again *[repeating the first four measures]*. . . . Now we go on to the second phrase . . . sixth chord (7) . . . *[continuing through the eighth measure]*. . . . The first phrase is then repeated—it *has* to be repeated, doesn't it? *[repeating the section]*. . . . It's interesting that in the whole structure you feel the urgency for the whole thing to be said again. . . .

That's how it should be played *[emphasizing the dissonance in the ornamentation by playing it firmly on the beat]*. . . . *[pausing and holding (8)]*. . . . Now that's the dominant of A minor (8). . . .

The second part begins *[playing briefly in the ninth measure]* . . . on the relative major, C. Already you see you've got a genius. You know it immediately. Anyone else would have stayed in E major, would have written the second part in E major. It's the natural, traditional thing to have done. But in this case we make a beautiful . . . harmonic tonal leap to C major *[outlining the concluding E-major chord (8) . . . and then continuing]*. . . .

Now with that embellishment (9) . . . we have this chord *[writing on the blackboard (9)]*, and in the next one (10), we have this chord:

(9)   (10)

Now this (10) is softer, isn't it? This is a minor seventh, this (9) is a major seventh. *[resumes playing at the ninth measure. . . . The configuration (9) is reiterated as an insistent rhythmic figure.]* . . . It was absolutely inevitable that the day would come when chords like these would become part of music, would be freed from tradition, would be taken out of harmony and become independent, expressive tonal entities. Absolutely logical.

[Resuming the Gavotte *at the ninth measure]*. . . . There (11), without any embellishment at all, absolutely naked and unadorned, this beautiful dissonance (11), a fifth and a minor seventh. . . . *[recommencing at (14)]* . . . there (12), he leaps into the major second *[emphasizing the descending leap . . . and plays D–E repeatedly]*. . . . Again (13) *[stressing the descending leap . . . repeating the major second E–F♯ several times . . . then proceeding to the end of the excerpt]*. . . .

Playing to emphasize "ugliness"

Now if you hear this played *[commencing at the beginning and playing much of the example in an expressively bland, metronomically smooth pianism]*, as you so often do, it's so pretty. *[The students laugh as they get the point.]* There is no awareness of what Gertrude Stein called so beautifully the "ugliness" that is always there in a piece of contemporary art. It's bound to be, because there must be the tension. And the tension is the ugliness, which we get so used to it's no longer ugly; the tension completely disappears. So we don't know what the composition is about anymore. We've lost the key to it.

This beautiful conclusion *[commencing at (14) and articulating the harmonic tensions]* . . . you've got to play that way! *[emphasizing the dissonance at (11) . . . and continuing]*. . . . You can do this with all the feeling of a gavotte and the movement of the dance . . . and (15) here is another one, *[stressing the dissonance in the chord . . . then continuing to the conclusion]*. . . .

You will find that all through the music of that period—Rameau, Couperin—the tension was created mostly by the ornaments, the embellishments, whatever word you're accustomed to using.[1] Created by the turns and the trills, and by prepared nonchordal tones—you follow me with that? Here, in Rameau (14) . . . the C is already there *[in the melody; the C is repeated]* . . . it's a consonance here. . . . There (11) . . . it becomes a dissonance. So it has been prepared beforehand by being a consonance, or a relaxation, then the tension is brought to bear by the harmonies that come underneath this prepared tone. Then you have the resolution to relaxation again. Is that clear to everybody?

Superimposing a seventh over the tonic

I think I mentioned earlier in talking about the dominant sevenths, in how much music of the late seventeenth and early eighteenth centuries you have the dominant chord:

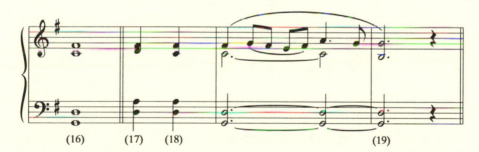

(16)   (17)   (18)   (19)

. . . over the tonic tone (16) . . . *[emphasizing the G by repeating it several times]* . . . *[repeating the chord and resolving to a G-major chord]*. . . . That, too, can be prepared *[playing the five–one cadence so that the dissonant F♯ is heard first as a consonance in D major (17) . . . then in the D dominant seventh chord (18) . . . then as a dissonance over a G bass . . . before finally resolving upward through a turn to G major (19)]*. . . .

This lovely dissonant effect, this tension, is created by putting the dominant *[repeating the dominant-over-tonic chord and emphasizing the tonic in the bass]* . . . over the tonic to which the whole chord will resolve. It's also possible to do that with the diminished seventh chord. Let's just keep all these chords in mind *[at the blackboard]*, because these are really the chords that are going to come. We have found them in Rameau, who died sometime in the eighteenth century. Now from the eighteenth century, you find these seventh chords very freely used in the late nineteenth and early twentieth centuries. So in just that space of time, these became independent harmonic entities, and the whole shift of tension moves from the tension of a tone in its relationship to the harmony, to the entire harmony.

---

[1] It is illuminating that the term "mordent," denoting turns incorporating major or minor seconds (several have been played in this example), originates in the Latin *mordere,* to bite.

Now, to get back to the diminished seventh chord:

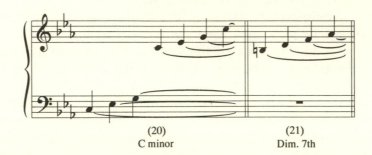

(20)
C minor

(21)
Dim. 7th

Here we are in C minor (20) *[arpeggiating the chord].* . . . The diminished seventh chord is (21) *[arpeggiated].* . . . When you play the diminished seventh chord over the tonic chord as Bach does in the beginning of this partita, you get such a sound as this:

(31)

EXAMPLE 13-4. J.S. Bach, *Sinfonia* from *Partita in C Minor*, opening.

. . . *[pausing at (22)]*. . . . Marvelous tension there! (22). . . . There it is—there's the C *[the bass note of the chord]*; there's the diminished seventh *[the four notes above it]* . . . *[recommencing]*. . . . He likes it; he does it again (23). . . . Now let's have seventh chords (24) . . . (25). . . . See what Bach does with seventh chords (26) . . . beautiful tension. And the relaxation is with a sixth chord (27) . . . it's with an inversion. . . . The D♭ against the C (28) *[reiterated several times]*. . . . All six-four chords (29) . . . (30) . . . and now the final (31) . . . resolution and relaxation. . . .

Marvelous isn't it, how this builds from this chord (22) . . . *[played several times]* which is closed and tight. We have just one third here *[playing the third in the treble]* . . . the whole diminished seventh in the left hand with the tonic tone. . . . Now the final seventh (31), we have a whole diminished seventh in the right hand . . . three more tones doubled below it over the G . . . *[playing (31) to the end of the measure]*. . . .

Look at the music you know, and look at the music you're studying, and think of this and have these ideas in the back of your mind. Learn to add tension and take it back again; to bring more urgency into your harmonic structure, and less urgency; to keep a complete resolution of tension away from the child if you feel he needs it. Because a complete resolution—if you're going in the middle of a session *[playing a simple major triad]* . . . it can end everything: his involvement, your grasp of the situation, his participation. And then it's time to say goodbye, isn't it?

Unprepared nonchordal tones

Now in Mozart we find that he very often uses the unprepared nonchordal tone. Now we've previously had the dissonant tone prepared. Think of this A-major sonata of Mozart with its beautiful variations in the very first movement. You know it:

continued on next page

continued from preceding page

EXAMPLE 13-5. Mozart, *Piano Sonata in A Major*, K. 331,
part of the principal theme and the beginning of the first variation.

[Playing measures five through eight of the principal theme]. . . . All right, the first variation
(32) . . . *[emphasizing the unprepared nonchordal melodic tones at (32) and (33)]* . . . then we
relax *[melodic chordal tones at (34)]* . . . urgency again (35). . . . *[continuing to (36) and (37)
and repeating them]*. . . . That (36) sounds like a little resolution of tension, and then you get
(37) . . . the seventh all by itself. . . . *[The piece is continued with the melody playfully chanted
to indicate the continuous sixteenth-note rhythm.]* . . . It's fantastic what lives there!

And what do you hear people do? *[demonstrating the variation played in a hasty
superficial manner that lacks any recognition of the significance of the nonchordal tones]*. . . .
No attention paid at all to this beautiful movement of urgency, of tonal direction
*[recommencing the variation in a detached, clearly articulated style, with emphasis on tonal
directions in the melody, and on the nonchordal tones]*. . . . How this thing wants to move,
and how it pulls your ear along—your whole being goes along with it!

And then I must bring in, someday, the *F Major Sonata,* because of the slow movement.
That marvelous slow movement in which there is such a complete tonal freedom—suddenly
you don't know what key you're in. You don't know what he's doing.

EXAMPLE 13-6. Mozart, *Piano Sonata in F Major*, K. 533, second movement, opening.

It begins *[playing to (38), holding the tones]* . . . with the most beautiful creative leap a man ever made. You couldn't top it *[recommencing . . . playing to (39), where the dissonance between the first note in the embellishment and the held B♭ in the left hand is stressed and repeated]* . . . beautiful B♭ and B♮. . . . *[continuing to (40) and emphasizing the octave C in the left hand under the tied F–D sixth (45) in the right].* . . . Where are we? *[continuing on to (41)].* . . . Fantastic! *[emphasizing the nonchordal E♭ bass octave against the tied D–F third in the treble].* . . . Here is a slow movement that has such intensity, all the way through.

If you do have Mozart sonatas, I almost implore you all to look at this one and just see what goes on. Study the use of the sixth chords *[beginning the movement again]* . . . the first two come here, sixth (42) . . . and sixth (43). . . . Now this wonderful unprepared dissonant chord (38) . . . ! *[continuing]* . . . Sixth (44). . . . And now we have . . . the intervals of the sixth (45) . . . sixth chord (46) . . . sixth chord (47). . . . We have the thirds (48) . . . that were in the left hand . . . *[plays into measure nine].* . . .

I have spent hours studying just this slow movement to see all that this creative genius probably wrote in half an hour. And how the mind worked, how the tonal laws—if they were not obeyed—were springboards into creative freedom.

Unprepared chords; silences; dynamics; harmonic progressions

Now with Beethoven—and of course this has to be so brief; we could spend a week on this study—with Beethoven, we find again unprepared nonchordal tones, and unprepared chords, as in these wonderful deceptive cadences. We find marvelous things happening in here, because we also have tension created by silence in this slow movement.

continued on next page

continued from preceding page

EXAMPLE 13-7. Beethoven, *Piano Sonata in E-flat Major,* op. 7, second movement, opening.

. . . *[beginning the movement, pausing in the rests]* (49). . . . What's going to happen (50) . . . ? Now what (51) . . . ? We wait again. . . . Ah! Now he holds that dissonance (52) . . . tension (53) . . . tension again here (54) . . . again here (55) . . . again here (56) . . . *[continuing]*. . . . Beautiful sevenths, dominant sevenths (57) . . . *[pausing in the rest]* (58), it's just electrifying what goes on with nothing happening . . . and now (59) . . . *[leading into the crescendo]* . . . diminished seventh (60), that wonderful tension . . . and tension with dynamics (61).

This is *his* particular genius, isn't it? The tension with dynamics; the tension with the building up to tension. How beautifully he prepares the tension and introduces it. The tension in silences. The momentary tensions that come with this A (55) *[repeating the D–A–B dissonance]* . . . and the A becomes an A♭ (56) . . . *[then playing the relaxation at the conclusion of the phrase in measure eight]*. You've got—the only word I can think of—you have a *poignant* tension.

You go to a sonata that begins as simply as this. C minor:

continued on next page

continued from preceding page

EXAMPLE 13-8. Beethoven, *Piano Sonata in C Minor,* op. 10, no. 1, opening.

. . . *[pausing at (62)].* All right, just the tones of the C-minor chord. Now we play it again (63) . . . together . . . *[continuing to (64)].* . . . Sounds very harmless, very charming, very gay. It's got minor, but the rhythm is gay *[singing the rhythm].* And he finishes the first subject.

[recommencing at (65) and playing through the rest of first subject . . . beginning the second subject (66)] . . . (67). Beautiful . . . first the single tone *[E♭]* (66) . . . then the tension comes *[D♭]* (67) . . . *[continuing to the end of the phrase].* . . . Now he repeats it without the first tone (68) . . . he starts immediately with the tension . . . third time (69) . . . *[continuing to the end of the excerpt].* . . . Beautiful dissonances in there, wonderful tensions *[recommencing the passage at (69) . . . emphasizing particular tensions through repetition: chords D♭–F–A♭–G♭ (70) and B♭–F–E♭ (71)].* . . .

That's the marvelous, glorious ugliness of Beethoven, which so very few people know how to put in it when you're listening to it. When they do, you know you're hearing a living performance. You don't really know why, but this is one of the reasons why. It's played with all this awareness of what lived in it for him as he composed it.

Now, for us to get some of this in our fingers, so that when we're improvising for a child we can bring in tension, release it, bring it in, deepen it, intensify it. Use tones that have an urgency to go somewhere. This little dominant-tonic exercise of mine *[Example 13-2]*, which you see work all the time with child after child—it's fantastic—it's just an indication. This is the simplest form of what a child can experience as tension.

So we can state that in Beethoven, we find—so beautifully and simply—his tensions come in his silences; his tensions are beautifully built up, marvelously achieved through harmonic progressions. His tensions can be momentary.

The momentum of a composition

And then you go a little bit later, and you come to Brahms. And with Brahms you find yourself in still another world. You find the chord itself in a rather transitional state.

Brahms was naturally trained as a classicist, as all classic composers were in those days. He studied counterpoint; he studied harmony; he studied the works of Mozart; he studied the works of Haydn. So he had all that tradition behind him. And this made it possible for him, in his chord progressions, to move his voices very logically and beautifully. And yet there is a tremendous amount of tension achieved just the same. For instance, in this intermezzo:

continued on next page

continued from preceding page

EXAMPLE 13-9. Brahms, *Intermezzo in E Major,* op. 116, no. 6, opening.

. . . *[pausing on the second chord and holding it]* (72). . . . Let's just pause on that. Isn't that beautiful? (73). . . . *[playing through the intermezzo with repetitions of particular chords of tension . . . (73) . . . (74) . . . and (75)].* . . . Sorry, when I play them out of tempo to illustrate, I get mixed up. *[recommencing, and playing without pause until (75)].* . . . Maybe I can now go on *[improvises an ending]* . . . something like that.

Sybil: Which one is that, Paul?
Paul: That's in opus 116. There are two extremely beautiful intermezzi in that
             opus. They're both in the key of E major. The other one begins with a
             triplet:

EXAMPLE 13-10. Brahms, *Intermezzo in E Major*, op. 116, no. 4, opening.

. . . [pausing at (76)] . . . lovely, that B♯. [recommencing and holding the chord with the B♯]. . . . It can only go where it wants to go [resolving the B♯ to C♯ . . . continuing to (77). . . . This chord (E–B–F♯–A) is taken out of the context of the intermezzo and repeated insistently in a rapid staccato manner, and contrasted with a higher dissonant chord]. . . . The chords, the chords you get! There's another marvelous chord, the kind of chord Stravinsky's going to use absolutely freely *[writing (77) on the blackboard],* that now come within an entire progression of chords. Now it's not achieved by the movement of one voice, it's achieved by the whole harmony. *[recommencing just after (76) and continuing through (79)].* . . . Wonderful two against three in that measure (78). There again, you have a tension achieved rhythmically. This is coming into music now.

. . . . (79) Relaxation . . . (80) tension . . . (81) relaxation . . . (82) tension . . . (83) tension . . . (84) tension . . . (85) a moment of relaxation . . . *[concluding with a restatement of the opening triplet motif].* . . .

Beautiful. It ebbs and flows in Brahms. It has almost a feeling pattern. You begin to move inside with this. It's quite different from the Beethoven building up to the tension. It's a tension that comes and goes and ebbs and flows, and that inside you're stirred by—you're tightened and let go, if you know what I mean, over and over and over and over.

And if you look carefully—I shouldn't take the time to tell you this—but the long melodic lines of Brahms are almost always composed of very short phrases. You have it here . . . *[playing the sequence of falling intervals in the treble (76) to (78)].* . . . You have it here . . . *[brief excerpts from Brahms* Intermezzo in B-flat Minor, *op. 117, no. 2, and* Intermezzo in E Minor, *op. 116, no. 5].* . . . A long melodic line of very short phrases was Brahms's particular genius.

Tonal fluidity

With Schumann we find a loosening of the establishment of key. By that I mean he doesn't start in the key, or start on the tonic or the dominant of the key, in which the composition is written. You have now a loosening of tonal feeling beginning. You get some of that in Beethoven, but on a very simple level. Beethoven began something—or does begin—on the dominant seventh occasionally, which was very shocking at the time. And I think in the *Ninth Symphony* there is a place where there is a thirteenth chord, and every tone of the scale is in that particular chord in the last movement. So he was very daring harmonically.

But now with Schumann, this lovely *Davidsbündler* I was telling you about only the other day: what happens in the very first piece? You're in G major:

EXAMPLE 13-11. Schumann, *Davidsbündler*, op. 6, no. 1, opening.

. . . *[playing from the beginning and pausing at (86)]* . . . so now you've gone to the dominant of E—in the very first phrase. What happens? . . . (87) He goes back to G, and immediately leaves it (88) . . . and comes back again (89) . . . *[leaves it again . . . and then returns to it]* (90). . . .

So now you begin to get in the nineteenth century this wonderful playing around with tonality. Composers just walk from one key into another inside of a few measures, like going through doors into different rooms. It's so exciting to see this. And this creates—again, it's another way of creating, a new way of creating—tension.

Here is a piece in B minor that begins with the dominant ninth *[arpeggiating the chord F#–A#–C#–E–G]* . . . this way:

EXAMPLE 13-12. Schumann, *Davidsbündler,* op. 6, no. 2, opening.

[Playing from the beginning] . . . Wonderful sound . . . B minor, it's a sixth chord (91) . . . the dominant (92) . . . the dominant ninth (93). . . . That's where we know where we are *[the B-minor configuration at the first ending].* . . . And back we go *[repeating only the first measure]* . . . and the second time *[going directly to the second ending and playing the following measure].* . . . You remember that wonderful example of what the change of one harmony can do *[Example 9-2, pages 81–82].* Well, there are so many of these that you should all study.

This is one of the most exciting things he ever wrote. It starts *[D–F♯]* . . . on a major third:

continued on next page

continued from preceding page

EXAMPLE 13-13. Schumann, *Davidsbündler*, op. 6, no. 7, opening.

. . . *[continuing to (94)].* Now for the first time we have eighth notes in an entire measure in the melodic line . . . (95) now we're on the dominant of G. . . . *[disregarding the repeat]* (96) We go to B-flat . . . *[playing to (97) and repeating the widely spaced chord]* . . . another one worth writing down. Fantastic chord!

This is Schumann—he's not letting the tension go, you see. *[recommencing in the G dominant seventh tonality two measures before (97)].* . . . We've gone to the dominant seventh of C minor . . . and now the second part ends on that *[D major]* chord (98) . . . and the first part begins on the same chord. Now this is like a beautiful piece of carpentry in which two pieces have been put together and you can't see any joining line. So you have a one—wait a minute—*[starting at (97), playing and singing-counting the descending melodic line into the cadence that leads into the recapitulation of the opening statement]*—one, two, three. . . . At the same time you have: *[starting at (97) again, and emphasizing the tenor voice, D–E♭–D, which, at (98), leads smoothly into the opening statement]* . . . we're back . . . and now a new rhythm *[playing and singing the dotted quarter note figure at (99) and continuing to the end of the phrase (102)].* . . . He still has something to say rhythmically. This hasn't happened before: *[playing from (99)]* . . . a dotted quarter . . . an eighth . . . and a quarter . . . and now the first sixteenth note comes, on this chord (100) *[repeating the chord, emphasizing its tension . . . then singing and playing the sixteenth note at (101)].* . . . Isn't that wonderful! *[repeating the recapitulation of the opening phrase].* . . . That leap of an octave (99) . . . ! That . . . melodic octave. *[continuing to the cadence at (102)].* . . . And the final phrase . . . *[stops at (103)].* Oh, I'm sorry, that's very hard, let's do that again *[repeats the final phrase].* . . . That dominant seventh (103) has tremendous tension, because it wasn't conceivable.

And the one you like so much, Jenny, which also comes from this *Davidsbündler,* in which there is no tonality at all:

continued on next page

continued from preceding page

EXAMPLE 13-14a. Schumann, *Davidsbündler*, op. 6, no. 9, first eighteen measures.

. . . *[playing energetically]*. . . . (104) What . . . key . . . are . . . we . . . in . . . ? C major (105) . . . ! But you leave it so fast—you leave it so fast, and off he goes . . . ! (106) Middle voice . . . (107) top voice . . . (108) low voice . . . (109) two voices . . . ! *[pausing at (110)]* But on the dominant seventh he does this *[plays the measure, stressing the dominant seventh harmony throughout]* . . . listen to that! *[omitting the next six measures]*

And in the coda, he still has something to say:

(113)

EXAMPLE 13-14b. Schumann, *Davidsbündler*, op. 6, no. 9, coda.

. . . [plays and repeats the first measure of the coda, then repeats the dissonance (111) with detached emphasis]. . . . And this one *[playing and repeating (112) forcefully and freely . . . then alternating the two chords for contrast]. . . .* And this one! *[repeating chord (113) sforzando]. . . .* Marvelous!

Clive: These sound like Gershwin chords out of context!

Paul: They're just fantastic! All done with these absolutely *[playing (112) freely and vigorously] . . .* cross-relations.[2] *[playing through the coda, freely repeating and stressing the dissonance and tension in selected chords . . . as the composition is brought to its conclusion]. . . .* Glorious piece of music!

Chromaticism in chord progressions

And then we go later in the nineteenth century—we can't finish today, I see—and we get to someone like César Franck. And we get into the chromaticism in which complete chords themselves are being used to create very quick alternations of tension and relaxation. You get sometimes in César Franck harmonies changing on the four beats of the bar, and not in a slow tempo—which you might encounter in Schumann, for instance.

On the other hand, with Franck, all these things that have happened are being carried forward. The loosening of tonality is now accepted in music. It's part of the composer's equipment, and he goes on with it. The using of nonchordal tones—of unprepared nonchordal tones—became an absolutely accepted part of music, just as these "old chords" became the chords of our contemporary music.

---

[2] It was impossible to transcribe the speech during this passage.

Really, it's knowing such things in your musical souls—they will have an influence on your improvisation. It will take a little time, because you need your growth time, and each one's growth time is different. But as long as your ears are keen and you keep these ideas when you're having a musical experience, you will be feeding your own "music child," which is going to serve the "music children" in our children.

Okay, let's do "Thank you for the music":

EXAMPLE 13-15. Nordoff, *Thank You.* From P. Nordoff and C. Robbins, *The Third Book of Children's Play-Songs* (Bryn Mawr, Pa.: Theodore Presser Co., 1980), p. 23. Used with permission.

. . . . *[The class joins in the song. When the part is reached where children are usually thanked by name, Clive, beginning with Schumann, inserts the names of composers whose works have been played in this exploration. The students are quick to pick up the idea, and as they sing, add composers of their choice. In this way, the esteemed composers are "thanked" for the gift of their music.]*

Thank you for the idea.

EXPLORATION FOURTEEN
MUSICAL ARCHETYPES, THE CHILDREN'S TUNE,
AND AN INTRODUCTION TO THE PENTATONIC

D efining the archetype, its bearing on racial inheritance, the collective unconscious, and its capacity to reach deeply into individuals. Musical idioms as archetypes: the children's tune, to which children respond universally, as a widely experienced example. The special therapeutic potential of archetypal musical idioms. The ethnomusicological and tonal interrelatedness of the principal culturally based idiomatic styles. The inadvisability of rigidly imposing nationalistic preferences in music therapy. Harmonizing the children's tune; organum chords as a source of stability; their similarity to ancient Chinese harmonization. The important research of Joseph Yasser into principles of pentatonic harmonization. Pentatonic harmony applied to the children's tune; the "dyad" and its role in pentatonic harmonization. The pentatonic as the harmonic foundation of the children's tune. Introducing the pentatonic modes. The creation of archetypes by other archetypes. The effects of chordal density and harmonic rhythm in harmonizing the children's tune. Further melodic and harmonic developments.

MUSICAL IDIOMS AS ARCHETYPES

What is an archetype?

Amanda: It's a universal concept.
Elaine: Something that relates to one thing which is constant in everybody—in their unconscious memory.
Paul: That's a little bit of it.
Jane H.: What is common to an awful lot of things at the same time.
Paul: That's a little bit of it.
Nancy: It's an experience or an interpretation.
Paul: It can be an experience. You can have an archetypal experience.

The dictionary meaning, the meaning that you should all know: it is a first form or model. In Jungian psychology an archetype is a pattern of thought, an image, a model that has been transmitted through generations and becomes part of the racial inheritance. And as part of the racial inheritance, these archetypes live in each one of us, in our souls, our subconscious selves—Jung would probably use the word "psyche"—they live there ready to be touched— this isn't Jung, now, this is an extension—ready to be touched or awakened by an experience that calls this forth, that touches on the deep memory.

Alfred: Would it help at all to quote Jung's own words?
Paul: Yes, please.
Alfred: He described it himself in his own words: "The primordial images which can be found in every human being."
Paul: Primordial images. How do they get to every human being?
Alfred: Because they go right back to the very beginnings of time immemorial.
Paul: And they are transmitted how?

Alfred: Into the psyche through, as you said, inheritance.
Jenny: Primordial images?
Alfred: In the collective unconscious. They are part of the collective
            unconscious—what Jung described as the collective unconscious.

THE CHILDREN'S TUNE AS AN ARCHETYPE

When we start working with idioms we are dealing with archetypes. The children's tune is certainly one of the strongest and one that doesn't lie very deep in the psyche. It swells out of children, springs out of children in their games, and when they are mocking each other, or calling to each other, or playing with each other. I don't know if you play "Ring Around the Rosie" in England—do you?—as we do in America.

[Assent from the students]

We play *[singing]* "Ring around the rosie, a pocket full of posie, da-da-da-da-da-da, ashes, ashes, we all"—the passing note that doesn't belong to the children's tune *[the note on "we"]*—"we all fall down." And we all fell down. Did you do that, too? Well, that's one of the very obvious ones.

Do you have such a game as that in Denmark or Norway?

[Assent from the students]

We can begin with the children's tune, which leads us directly into the pentatonic.

THE CONNECTIONS AMONG MUSICAL IDIOMS

[Writing on the blackboard] The pentatonic is very ancient. Pentatonic scales go back to at least 3000 B.C. and are probably still older than that. Pentatonics became altered in other countries: not by the Chinese, but by the Japanese, by the Greeks. In Europe, in A.D. as far as we know—it might have been B.C., too, to some extent—the modes were developing. We also find altered modes, and these are in our Middle Eastern scales, the scales of Turkey, of Syria, of all that region.

It's very interesting that we have Celtic pentatonics, from which organum developed. We have organum here—I'll just put it here in this scheme—because it connects the pentatonic with the Spanish idiom, particularly in Andalusia, where the music was most influenced by the Moors, by the Arabs. It's fascinating, isn't it, to see all of these connections? We have here the Scottish music. And out of the entire scheme we have all of the folk song, folk music, which has its connections everywhere.

ARCHETYPAL IDIOMS AND THEIR INTERRELATEDNESS

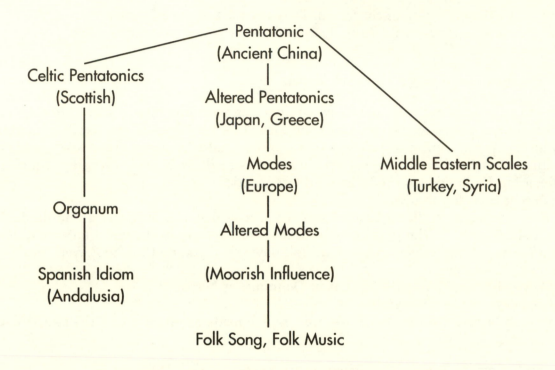

REACHING BEYOND RACE AND CULTURE FOR THE UNIVERSAL

Now I have met one or two music therapists who have strongly the idea that children should only be given the folk music—or music similar to the folk music—of the country in which they were born. You've heard of that, have you? I think this is so terribly narrow, that you give a child born in Russia only Russian folk music—or that kind of music—as therapy. Of course, this is therapy they're talking about. Or a child in Israel gets that kind of music, a French child would get French folk music, and so on. You really can't hold such a narrow view as that.

Nancy: Paul, you said, kind of, in your introduction, at the beginning, there was
          an implication that different races have different archetypes—different
          archetypal music—
Paul: I should think they would, yes.
Nancy: Yet, as we're talking now, it seems to me that a child of one race
          responds to the archetypes of many races.
Paul: Aha! Now you've put your finger right on it, haven't you? Why should
          this be?
Jenny: That, as an archetype, it is independent of race.
Jane H.: In the child, you're reaching quite beyond the culture, so that what
          you're dealing with is not culturally dependent at all. So the child may
          be. . . .

Paul: Yes, but I think we can't use the word "culture," because the archetypes
          go back so many thousands of years—actually to the beginning of time
          and the creation of the world, some of them.

This is the thing one has to think about very seriously in working with these archetypes.
Why should an African-American child respond as he did to a tango? Why should the son of
an American respond as he did to a Middle Eastern scale, so consistently and extraordinarily
that he actually in one session—we have a picture of him—began dancing with his hands
held above his head like this *[moving in a style directly suggestive of a sinuous belly dance]*
and moving like this around the drum to this music? This was an autistic child who began
his first session as far away from the piano as he could get, and finished up singing songs
with me.
     You're finding the music that reaches the chord in that child's psyche—or the string—
that wants to vibrate, and this idiom sets it vibrating and starts the response.

HARMONIZING THE CHILDREN'S TUNE

So, let us begin with our first archetype *[writing on the blackboard]*. And can we sing it? Give
me a G, Jane!

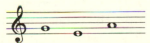

EXAMPLE 14-1. The "first archetype," the tones of the children's tune.

[Throughout the exploration the students sing all the examples on "ah."] . . . Again *[the tones
are sung again, more slowly]*. . . . Now sing as I point:

[The class is directed to sing the notes in differing orders and repetitions.] . . .

Alfred: I'm back in my Chinese temple!
Paul: The marvelous variety one can get with just three tones! Now let's put it
          in a rhythm *[writing on the blackboard]*, and Tom, will you come to the
          piano, please, and play it for us:

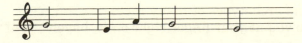

. . . . Good. Can we all sing it? *[The class sings the phrase.]* . . . Now only Tom sing it, please.
And, Tom, sustain this through the whole four measures *[writing out the sustained
accompanying interval G–C in the treble (1)]*. Play this on the piano and sing the tune
against it:

EXAMPLE 14-2. The children's tune, with piano accompaniments made up of fourths and fifths.

[Tom sings the tune on the syllable "ah" with accompaniment (1).] . . .

Good, again *[the exercise is repeated on the syllable "la"].* . . . Good, now *[writing in middle C (2)]* change your chord and add this, and sustain it through *[Tom repeats the exercise, with (2) added to (1) in the accompaniment].* . . . Interesting what doubling the C does to the tune, isn't it? Once more, Tom, and focus your singing to a child *[the exercise is repeated].* . . . Very nice. Now add this to it in the bass *[the exercise is repeated with the addition of (3)]* . . . and this *[(4) is added to the accompaniment].* . . . Each one is a different experience. Let's hear them all one after the other, Tom. First these two *[(1)]*; these three *[(1) and 2)]*; and then these *[(3) in the bass clef added]*; and finally that *[(4) added].* All right? *[Tom sings the exercise through, adding the tones of (3) separately, thus making five versions of the accompaniment].* . . . Good. Now take the last one and let's sing it very softly. *[Tom repeats the last version softly as the group begins to join in the singing.]* . . . Again *[the example is repeated].* . . .

ORGANUM, THE CHILDREN'S TUNE, AND CHINESE MUSIC

It's a very beautiful experience, and all we have here are chords made of fourths and fifths. May we note that is a chord we call what?

Jane H.:   Organum.
Paul: Organum chord. And the organum chord then has its origin in Chinese music, where our interval of the fourth is their interval of the third. Their harmonies are built on fourths, as ours are built on thirds. All right, Tom, thank you very much. Now what would the experience of this *[organum chord]* be? How would you describe it? Would this be—? Well, tell me.
Elaine: An outward-going experience supported by the ego experience.
Paul: By a what?
Elaine: By the ego experience of the open fifth and the octave.
Paul: Yes, yes, good. And emotionally, what kind of an experience would you think it to be for a child?

Students: Secure.

Paul: Secure. Stable, isn't it? This one harmony supports the archetypal melody and you have a stable experience. Tom, come back. Do you mind? We haven't finished with it yet. Do it again, softly, repeating the chord when you come here *[indicating the beginning of the third measure],* all right? Start again from the top. Perhaps, Jane, you'll sing this time.

Jane H.:   Yes, sure.

Paul: From where you are. Tom, play for Jane:

[Tom playing accompaniment (1) as Jane sings the melody]. . . . Good! Now the octave . . . *[The successive developments of the accompaniment are played.]* . . . and now with the bass. . . . But you must repeat the chord on the G *[third measure].* Once more. . . . Again, with the next one. *[(3) is added, then 4).]* . . .

Now, my feeling is this *[the repetition of the chord]* gives it even more security.

[To Jane] That's the best singing I've ever heard you do. That's how you must sing to your child. I'm delighted to hear you sing like that. Beautiful!

The repetition of the chord simply strengthens the feeling of stability, doesn't it? And it gives an added support to the archetype.

Now let's do it: *[singing to indicate a tempo almost four times faster]* la la-la la la—as fast as that—and play on da da-da da da—four times *[repeating the organum chord on every beat].* Amanda, you sing:

. . . . *[The phrase is repeated beginning with the interval of the fourth in the right hand; in each repetition the chord is built by the addition of the next lower tone, making five stages in the development of the accompaniment.]*

Amanda, I'm a little child standing here and you're singing to me. Go on, sing to me! Let it come out on your breath *[demonstrates stronger singing]:* ah ah-ah ah ah! Come on! *[Amanda begins to sing with more conviction to the repeated accompaniment.]* Open your mouth! . . . Wider! . . . Yes! Wasn't it better when she opened her mouth?

Students: *[agreeing and supportive]* Yes!
Amanda: It was my throat that I opened. *[She sings the phrase strongly.]*
Paul: Well, you could open your throat because your mouth was open, too.

Now very lightly, and let's all do it, and Tom, you play it for them. *[The class sings the archetype lightly through the five versions of the accompaniment.]* Ja! How lovely that is! It's stimulating without any emotional pressure. It's arousing and quickening, and yet there is no pressure. Thank you, Tom.

FURTHER HARMONIC DEVELOPMENTS IN THE PENTATONIC

But now, we have a child, let us say, we want to give a little delicate "needling"—if I can put it like that—so we're going to make a harmonic change. And we're using pentatonic harmonies, naturally *[writing in the change in the harmonization]*, because, as Clive said earlier, this archetype is derived from the pentatonic scale. When we come to the pentatonic, you will see that two children's tunes make a complete pentatonic scale.

All right, Amanda, who just sang so beautifully. Would you come to the piano, please? And sing as you did before—open your mouth and your throat, and sing and play.

EXAMPLE 14-3. The children's tune, harmonized with two chords.

Ready? *[Amanda sings the melody boldly while playing (1). . . . At (5) the harmony changes to the interval E–A for a beat, then returns to G–C]. . . . Again! [Amanda repeats the phrase over the first form of the harmonization.]* . . . And now, with the octave added (2). . . . Isn't that nice, just that fleeting change? Once more, Amanda *[Amanda repeats, singing as she plays (1) and (2)]. . . . And now let's add a little more tone to it. Now let's do this one, Amanda [writing (3) on the blackboard]. . . . Beautiful. Now very softly, but still open [the third form of the reharmonization is repeated]. . . . Lovely! And add the octave here. . . . Now the interest here is in the change in harmonic rhythm. [Harmonic rhythm is the rhythm created by the progression of harmony, by the changes of chords.] We had no change in the harmonic rhythm at all in the first one. Here we have a very fleeting change, and it gives it a completely different character. Thank you, Amanda.*

THE PENTATONIC MODES

I think we have to touch briefly on the pentatonic, because it will make this harmonization so much more meaningful to you, and will connect it with the pentatonic, which we will be doing later *[Exploration Fifteen]*. Now Nancy, would you go to the piano, please, and play me a pentatonic starting on A *[Nancy plays A–B–C♯–E–F♯]. . . . That's right. Once more. [The scale is repeated.] . . .* Can we derive this *[the children's tune G–E–A]* from that pentatonic? Hm? *[Nancy plays G♯–E–A–G♯–E. . . . This phrase is not the "normal" children's tune and is in fact derived from an altered pentatonic scale.]*

First of all, what are the intervals we have here in this children's tune? We have a descending minor third *[G–E]*; we have a descending major second *[A–G]*; and we have the ascending perfect fourth *[E–A]*, right? Will you play the pentatonic from A again? *[As Nancy plays, the names of the notes are spoken]*: A, B, C♯, E, F♯. Where is the G? There's no G. Play the other form. *[The notes are named for Nancy to play]*: A, B, D, E, F♯. . . . There's no G. So you can't get this *[G–E–A]* child's tune—this children's tune—from a pentatonic on A. *[Although the G–E–A children's tune is not available in the first scale Nancy played, A–B–C♯–E–F♯, two other children's tunes are: E–C♯–F♯ and A–F♯–B. Two children's tunes are inherent in the tonal structure of every (unaltered) pentatonic scale, formed around the two augmented steps (steps of a minor third) that belong to the scale. Nancy's second scale, A–B–D–E–F♯, contains the children's tunes D–B–E and A–F♯–B. The second scale, as dictated to Nancy, introduces a different mode of the pentatonic to the first scale (see below).]*

Play a pentatonic on E *[directing Nancy, who plays E–F♯–G♯–B–C♯]. . . .* You have a G♯. Play the other form *[Nancy plays E–F♯–A–B–C♯]. . . .* You have no G. *[Again, although the G–E–A children's tune is not available in these scales, others are. The scale E–F♯–G♯–B–C♯ contains B–G♯–C♯ and E–C♯–F♯; the scale E–F♯–A–B–C♯ contains A–F♯–B and E–C♯–F♯. However, Paul Nordoff is apparently mindful of the need to return to his previously established tonality for the next step in his exploration; he bypasses any discussion of the children's tune correlations with these other scales, and continues guiding Nancy back to the G–E–A children's tune.]*

Play the pentatonic starting on G *[Nancy plays G–A–B–D–E]. . . .* They're all there, aren't they? G, E, and A. The other form: *[Nancy plays G–A–C–D–E]*:

EXAMPLE 14-4. Two forms of the pentatonic on G.

[These are two modes of the pentatonic, the first mode (a) and the third mode (b). In every key there are five modes of the pentatonic, each taking its name from the degree of the scale on which it is formed.] So G is the root tone of this children's tune, and, in the pentatonic on G, E would be the fifth tone, right? E is the dominant. *[See later references to the research by Joseph Yasser into pentatonic harmonization in* A Theory of Evolving Tonality.*]* A would be the second tone. Are you with me? So that in this pentatonic (a), or in this one (b)—we number the tones of the scale—E would then be the dominant in each case.

And you would have a dominant-tonic cadence—the chord on E followed by the chord on G, the chord on the fifth tone followed by the chord on the first tone. Now let's just do that with fourths, and we'll take this form (a), which I like better. It follows the outline of the tune exactly.

EXAMPLE 14-5. The children's tune, with harmonization using the first mode.

Jane, would you come to the piano, please. All right, Jane, sing in that lovely voice again.

Jane H.:   Sorry, just the top line?
Paul: Just the top line, yes. Sing this line, and play this. *[Jane sings and plays (1), the harmonization consisting of fourths on each note of the melody.]* . . . Again. *[The example is repeated.]* . . . Isn't it lovely?

One, five, two, one, five *[indicating the degrees of the scale upon which the chords are built]*, and that five makes you want to go back to the one and repeat it. So this is an endless archetype, isn't it? It can go on, and on, and on—and it is going on, and on, and on. If the children sang da da-da da da da *[singing the G–E–A–G–E of the children's tune and adding a final G, thereby returning the melody to the tonic of the mode]*, it would be quite another thing, wouldn't it? It wouldn't be the same experience at all. But this has no end. It just goes on, and on, and on, and on.

PENTATONIC DOMINANT-TONIC HARMONIZATION

Now let's add the octave to it Jane, all along. *[Jane sings as she reinforces the accompaniment by adding (2) to (1).]* . . . That's beautiful. Now let's add G and follow it through. *[(3) is added.]* . . . Beautiful. Now with the fifth *[(4) is added.]* . . . Now with the octave below, the G doubled. *[Jane sings as she adds (5) to the accompaniment, doubling the top note in each chord in the bass clef an octave below.]* . . . That's it.

Now let's all sing it, starting from the beginning. *[to Jane]* Just the top two. Faster. *[All sing with the first version of the accompaniment.]* . . . Softly. *[All sing softly.]* . . . Now with C and very slowly. *[The second form of the accompaniment is played.]* . . . With the G added. *[The third form of the accompaniment is played.]* . . . Now with the fifth added, and quickly again. *[All sing to the fourth form of the accompaniment.]* . . . Again! *[All sing.]* . . . Very softly again. *[All sing.]* . . . Good. And now with these *[bass tones]*, very slowly and with a big voice. *[The class sings to the complete form of the accompaniment.]* . . . More tone, Jane. Again. *[The final form is repeated.]* . . .

We have nobility in this, don't we, at that tempo? We have something that's like a processional, something that has a noble, ritualistic quality, when you use these doublings. When it's thin and light and delicate—you've got a change of harmony on each one—this can be so stimulating, so arousing for a child, an irresistible kind of archetypal experience. Thank you, Jane.

Sybil: There's the most fascinating—it's at the back of my mind, I must find it—wonderful, wonderful processional from one of the islands of Scotland. I'll find it for you.

Paul: Yes. This is where you find it exactly: in pentatonic music and this kind of harmony. Because, after all, what is the fifth but an inversion of the fourth? And these are the two intervals the Chinese have been using since the eleventh century.

KUBLAI KAHN AND THE PENTATONIC

Now this form of the scale:

. . . emphasizes the tonic triad, doesn't it? *[singing in the third mode form of the scale to emphasize that the first, third, and fourth degrees of the scale form a diatonic major triad in root position]* This form—according to Mr. Yasser, who has done tremendous research on this—persisted in China for centuries, until Kublai Khan changed it to this one:

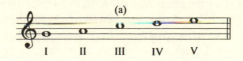

And it has remained in this *[first mode]* form to the present day. So that means for the last eight-hundred-odd years, or something like that. He was very musical, extremely sensitive, and wrote a treatise on the scale.

Nancy: Really!
Paul: Yes.
Knud: What was his name?
Paul: Kublai Khan, the Great King.

THE "DYAD" AS THE BASIS OF PENTATONIC HARMONY

Now just to show you something else that is so beautiful and fascinating. Let us erase this form (b), and confine ourselves to using the form (a) that does not emphasize the diatonic major chord. So we have these notes, and here we have the G, the E, and the A of this pentatonic. Now, the other one is *[singing C–A–D–C–A, turning to Example 14-5, and pointing to the transposition of the melody, line (2) in the harmony]* right there in the middle. Isn't it lovely?

So, two children's tunes *[playing G–E–A–G–E, the initial form of the melody]*: now, if you harmonize that in fourths *[above the melody]*, what do you get? The C, the A, and the D.

There's your complete pentatonic scale *[G–A–C–D–E]*. Isn't that lovely? How archetypal can you get! I mean these two archetypes create another archetype. Two archetypes can be derived from one.

Clive: I guess archetypes are like that.
Paul: Indeed, I'm afraid they are.

So there we have demonstrated that the correct harmonization—based on what Mr. Yasser calls "dyads," because those two tones in the pentatonic, a perfect fourth apart, take the place of the three in the diatonic that form the triad—the correct harmonization gives us the second children's tune and the complete pentatonic scale. *[Pentatonic harmonization is more fully discussed and demonstrated in Exploration Fifteen.]* It also works the same way if you use the other form (b). The notes are different then; you have to harmonize with fifths instead of fourths. The same thing happens.

Now, we have time to go just a step further. Does this interest you all?

Students: Yes, great!

Isn't it lovely to know this about the pentatonic? Then, when you begin to use it, to practice it, it will be so meaningful for you because you will know why it means so much to the children. It is part of their soul life; it is part of them. It is part of their music child. And very often it's just this that can arouse and awaken the music child. In a child who doesn't speak, a child who's very young, or a child who's autistic, this scale can do wonderful things.

FURTHER HARMONIC, RHYTHMIC, AND STYLISTIC ELABORATIONS

Now, let's go into a new key *[A–B–D–E–F♯]*, and we'll start with this one.

Elaine, we're going to sing the children's tune beginning on A, and we're going to sing it in this rhythm *[singing the melody in the rhythm of example]*, and you play *da da-da-da* da *[indicating where the chords of the accompaniment are played]*. Would you sing, please? *[Elaine sings and plays the example; on the repeat she sings the familiar melodic rhythm by changing the first quarter note of the melody to two eighth notes.]* . . . That's using just the one *[inverted]* and the five. Let's all sing it. *[The class sings the example as written.]* . . .

Now we're going to extend it.

EXAMPLE 14-6. The children's tune in the first mode on A.

And we're going to sing *[singing the added eighth note in the third measure]*, right? Elaine first, please. *[Elaine plays and sings the example with accompaniment (1).]* . . . Good. Everyone! *[All sing the example.]* It's much more playful in its character, isn't it, when you use the dominant so prominently.

Clive: We could hardly hear it when we were singing.
Elaine: Shall I double it?
Paul: Let's double it, Elaine. Yes. First with octaves, right?

[The additions to the accompaniment are written on the blackboard.] Okay, and we'll sing it more softly. *[The class sings, as Elaine plays (1) and (2), doubling the upper tone in each of the accompanying intervals.]* . . . Beautiful, isn't it? Elaine, you must sing more clinically.

Now we'll add our extra tone here *[adding the bass tone on the blackboard (3)]*. Ready? Elaine, you'll know it. *[The example is sung and played.]* . . . All right, now let's all sing it lightly. *[The class sings the example.]* . . .

All right, now we'll do something that I think you will like very much *[writing on the blackboard]*. There we are.

EXAMPLE 14-7. The children's tune, with a further accompaniment.

Let's sing it softly again, and you play with some strength. *[The example is played and sung.]* . . . Completely different experience. We do it once more. *[The example is repeated.]* . . . Good. Now, let's have gongs *[writing on the blackboard]*. Shall we have gongs?

EXAMPLE 14-8. The children's tune, with a gonglike bass.

All right, slow and majestic. Ready? *[The example is played, sung, and repeated.]* . . . You see, it never wants to stop! It wants to go on, and on, and on with a harmonization like this, a nice one to use when you want to activate a vocal response. *[For a further example of the "gong effect," see Exploration Fifteen, pages 162–163.]*

Nancy: Paul, the one before this one *[Example 14-7]* did stop things. Would that be used also, clinically? I felt very stopped by that, held by that one.

Paul: It would depend what you did with your voice.

Nancy: Yes.

Paul: It would be a good one to do—play this one *[the accompaniment of Example 14-8]* and hold this *[indicating the tonic chord in the third measure]* through the next measure, and let me sing it:

EXAMPLE 14-9. The children's tune, with a melodic variation.

See what I mean? You keep it going with your singing, and yet you give the child some harmonic stability for that moment.

Nancy: Yes!

Paul: Okay, Elaine, thank you.

INTRODUCING THE "CHINESE SEVENTH CHORD"

Now we can use—I'll be very daring now and skip a bit, and use a seventh chord. A Chinese seventh chord, of course. All right, Jenny. Still singing on A *[beginning to sing the melody]*. Or let's change the rhythm. *[sings phrases on "la"]* That's it *[writing the variation on the blackboard]*:

EXAMPLE 14-10. The children's tune, altered and harmonized using a Chinese seventh chord.

[Jenny sings the melody.] . . . Good. *[The example is sung twice, to accompaniment (1).]* . . . Isn't that beautiful? Let's see where the seventh chord is. *[In measure two, the dyad B–E forms a seventh chord (inverted) with the F♯ in the melody. In the fourth measure the B–E dyad also forms a seventh chord with the A in the melody.]* Can we all sing that—and play it in octaves, maybe? *[The class sings the example as Jenny plays accompaniment (1) plus (2).]* . . . Again *[the example is repeated]*, no mistakes. . . . Very softly. *[The example is repeated as directed.]* . . . Absolutely ravishing, isn't it? Just purely beautiful!

Now play the tonic, the subdominant, and the dominant of C major. *[Jenny begins the progression, then follows the naming of the chords.]* . . . The subdominant . . . dominant . . . tonic. . . . Now let's do this again: *[Example 14-10 is repeated.]* . . .

Fantastic difference, isn't it? How much more attractive this seems! You can see where this would appeal to the child, not only because it's his tune, but because the harmonies are right for his tune. And his music child is going to feel that these harmonies are right, that they're suitable. And they're not going to be—it's completely different from anything he hears on TV or records at home in the diatonic system, so it's going to be refreshing. It's going to be stimulating. It's going to be revivifying. I love this one *[Example 14-10]*. I think this is a very important one, a very good one to get into your fingers.

All right, thank you very much.

Students: Thank you.

EDITOR'S   *Paul Nordoff had known the musicologist Joseph Yasser personally and had worked with him in*
NOTE   *the early 1930s. Yasser was then publicizing his theory of evolving tonality, and Nordoff was a*
            student of composition at the Juilliard School of Music in New York. Yasser's proposal that the next
            logical stage in the evolution of music was the development of a nineteen-tone scale was stimulat-
            ing considerable interest in the musical world, both among artists and business interests, and there
            was a great deal of curiosity as to how it would sound. The Steinway piano company undertook
            to restring and tune a piano to a nineteen-tone scale, and Nordoff was asked to demonstrate it.

            Although he was intrigued by the melodic and harmonic subtleties possible in the new scale,
            it was Yasser's foundational research into the music of ancient China and the evolution of scales
            that most deeply stirred Nordoff's interest. This research clearly stated the relationship between

pentatonic scales (which Yasser termed "infradiatonic scales") and diatonic scales, and their distinctly different harmonic properties. Later, Nordoff was to combine this perception with Steiner's views on the pentatonic—with particular reference to the musical experiences of children—and with Steiner's interval concept, thus creating a theoretical foundation for the clinical application of the pentatonic in music therapy.

EXPLORATION FIFTEEN
PENTATONIC HARMONIZATION AND STYLES OF IMPROVISATION

*Y*asser's research into Chinese music as the basis for clinical improvisation using pentatonic harmonization. The additions of selected intervals and chords to bring a greater richness of tone color. The fourth, not the third, as the fundamental harmonic interval. Constructing the acceptable intervals on each scale tone to produce an extensive range of intervals; improvising with them to accustom the ear to the sound of the pentatonic. Why tonal directions in the pentatonic are less compelling than those in diatonic music, and more melodically than harmonically determined; the intervals that produce the greatest tensions in diatonic versus pentatonic music. The fifth scale tone as the dominant; forming the dominant harmony and cadences. Examples of two-, three-, and four-tone chords and how they are used in progressions and resolutions. Including "pentatonic seventh chords." Exercises and different styles in pentatonic improvisation. Barton, an example of clinical application. An experience of a Javanese gamelan. The inherent qualities of the pentatonic idiom. Examples of traditional pentatonic melodies harmonized diatonically and pentatonically. A Chinese folk song.

CLINICAL IMPROVISATION USING PENTATONIC HARMONY

I think I should tell you that the clinical use of the pentatonic has been developed by me, based on the harmonic construction of Joseph Yasser. He has given a textbook harmony of Chinese music. I've done the same thing with it that I have done with textbook harmony in the diatonic scale. I have taken from it the intervals that were used by the Chinese, and added intervals and chords that they actually did not use, because this gives the pentatonic a richness that otherwise it simply wouldn't have. We couldn't confine ourselves to the organum type of harmony which the Chinese used almost exclusively, particularly in their sacred music. What it's like now in China, of course, one doesn't know *[China was a closed country at the time of these lectures],* but at the time that Yasser's book was written all the religious music used only the fourths and the inverted fourth, which is the fifth, to harmonize their melodies, and it was only the secular music—the music of the people—in which you would find thirds.

HARMONIC THIRDS ARE INADMISSIBLE IN THE PENTATONIC

Let's take this form *[first mode on C]:*

If you are finding the basic interval for a chord in the diatonic scale, you do what?

Jean: Form it on the basic thirds on the tonic.

Paul: You omit a note, don't you? You go from C, you omit the D, and you go to an E. So if we apply the diatonic technique, which is what Yasser has done:

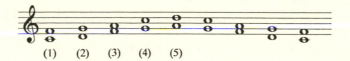

(1)   (2)   (3)   (4)   (5)

. . . our first interval would be that (1). Correct? *[Throughout this exploration the scales and intervals are written on the blackboard.]* Our second interval would be this (2), the third would be this (3), the fourth would be this (4), the fifth would be that (5). Now we have the correct way of finding the basic interval on which the harmony rests, and you see, we have four fourths. The major third is absolutely out, and if you can *train* yourself to omit that third in your improvisations, you will find this is one of the toughest disciplines you've ever had to do, but it's enormously rewarding.

Elaine: Could I ask a question, Paul?

Paul: Yes.

Elaine: Why is the major third there unacceptable, even though it's in the actual scale that we're using?

Paul: Because it's a dissonance. In this music, it is a dissonance. You see, this doesn't answer you, except intellectually, and it's terribly hard to conceive of this (3) as being a dissonant interval.

FORMING INTERVALS ON EACH TONE OF THE SCALE

Sissel, would you play them, please? Play the scale alone first, slowly and firmly so we all have it in our heads:

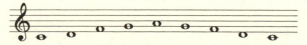

[Sissel plays the scale ascending and descending.] . . . Lovely, now let's play the basic intervals:

[The intervals are played ascending and descending.] . . . You can really begin to hear this (3) as dissonance in this harmonic structure. These two tones *[indicating the fourths at (1), (2), (4), and (5)]* take the place of a three-tone diatonic chord. Yasser actually calls them dyads instead of triads. Play it once more, Sissel, because I do think your ear can begin to hear that third as a dissonance. . . . It becomes more and more clear, doesn't it, that the third simply doesn't belong. Now if we form the intervals on the ground tone C *[writing on the blackboard]:*

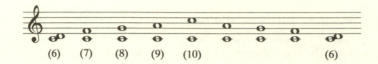

. . . we have a major second (6), which the Chinese also do not use, we have the fourth again (7), we have the fifth (8), we have the sixth (9) which *is* acceptable, and of course, we have the octave (10).

Now let's hear the intervals on the ground tone, the tonic tone, C *[ascending]*. . . . Now the sixth (9) does not offend the way the third did, because of the space that is between the two tones—and down. . . . Now this major second (6), which the Chinese do not use, we *do* use clinically.

All right, let's take the intervals from the second tone, D. You make them for us, Sissel:

. . . . There again, you feel how incongruous that particular third is. Play both groups now, Sissel. Just go up this group *[ascending from C],* and then go up this group *[ascending from D].* . . . Good!

Now let's form them on the next tone, F. Just take the notes of the scale as they come, with the F as the ground tone each time. We've done the first degree, second degree, now we're going to do the third degree. So the first would be F–G:

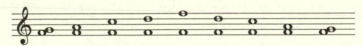

. . . that's right . . . and also, you can always have the octave, can't you, because that's a possibility. All right, play that one up and down . . . good. . . . Then this one *[indicating D–A, and leading Sissel through a succession of intervals].* . . . Begin to get your ear oriented, and some feeling and idea of how these intervals will sound when they're used freely. Now we have two more tones—we have the subdominant; we begin on G:

. . . . Good. Play them down. . . . *[then indicating a further series of intervals for Sissel to play].* . . . Good! Thank you. Now on the dominant *[A]:*

. . . *[The A–C third is played.]* Sounds strange, doesn't it? The third begins to sound strange every time you come back to it. *[Sissel continues.]* . . . Good. Play them up and down. . . . Good. Now let's play the octaves. *[Sissel follows as they are pointed out; the directing again leads into a succession of freely chosen intervals.]* . . . That's it. Good! Thank you very much.

We have a tremendous number of possible intervals to use. Many more than you think, perhaps, more than you would have suspected.

THE PENTATONIC EXCLUDES THE INTERVALS OF GREATEST TENSION

[Writing out the tritone C–F♯] That you will never find in a pentatonic, a normal pentatonic—the tritone that brings the tension into diatonic harmony—that brings the tension into the dominant seventh—that has the *direction* to *move* to the tonic. There is *no* tritone present here in any of the chords we have. What do we have? *[indicating intervals on the blackboard]* We have the perfect fourth. We have the perfect fifth. We have the sixth—in this case the major sixth. We have the octave. We have the major sixth. We have the fifth. We have the major second—there is no minor second. Major second, fourth, fifth. We have a minor seventh: minor seventh—there is no major seventh. So you don't have the tension of the direction of a tone wanting to move:

(11). . . . You don't have the tension of (12) . . . this wanting to resolve to C–E . . . or (13) B♭–G♭ . . . at least to move. These you don't have. You don't have this kind of tone *[minor second]* with this direction (14) . . . or (15). . . . It's nonexistent. So that there is no tritone, no minor second, no major seventh. These came later when the pentatonic scale underwent its changes and alterations.

Clive: You don't have those—and they are the diatonic intervals of tension, aren't they?
Paul: Yes.
Clive: And you don't have the diatonic intervals of balance, either—the thirds.
Paul: No. For instance, where the tritone should go—could go—to a third, you don't have this. The minor second could go to—well, it also wants to go to a third, really, primarily, so there again, the third isn't available. The major seventh can go to the octave.

IMPROVISING FREELY WITH THE ADMISSIBLE INTERVALS

Now, will someone come and take—let's see, whose turn is it? Unni. Just play freely among these permitted intervals. *[Unni comes to the piano and plays a succession of intervals]:*

. . . . Good. Now, while you're doing that, do that in the left hand *[indicating the intervals on the board]* and play a free melody in the scale in your right. Can you? Can you see?

Unni: Yes:

. . . . Good, Unni. Very nice, very nice. Thank you very much. Now we need a few guidelines, obviously, a few guidelines as to how to use these intervals so that they would be most effective. When, for instance, you use the second, resolve it nicely. Resolve it as one would in diatonic harmony with the feeling for the direction of the tone.

TONAL DIRECTIONS AND RESOLUTIONS

Jean, why don't you come back, and let's do a little more work:

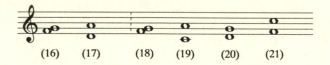

Play these resolutions: (16) . . . (17). . . . Good, repeat (16) . . . (17) . . . and the next one (18) . . . (19). . . . Now if you do that, you then should do this (20) . . . , and this (19) becomes a kind of passing harmony between the second and the fourth. Can we do this again? *[Jean repeats the resolutions . . . then repeats (18) . . . (19) . . . (20).]* . . . Complete this one (21). . . . Good. This would be very nice—these are just examples of harmonic progressions.

RESOLVING THE DOMINANT: THE FIFTH SCALE TONE

Now Jean, let's take the dominant chord, the dominant dyad:

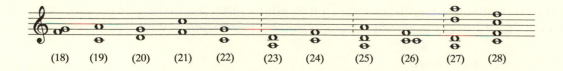

(23) . . . (24) . . . *[repeats the cadence].* . . . That's it. Now would you play it from here *[(18) . . . playing the intervals indicated in succession to (24)].* . . . Once more . . . , hold it (23) . . . *[pause; then completes the phrase (24)].* . . . That's it, now once more *[repetition].* . . . Yes. This is a pentatonic cadence (23)–(24) and it's possible to extend it so that it would look like this (25)–(26).

Can we play this again? And this time we'll go to the second cadence. *[playing (18) through (22) and adding (25)–(26)].* . . . Now play five-seven to one in any diatonic scale. *[Jean obliges in C major.]* . . . Now play this again (25)–(26). . . .

Jane H.:   It's interesting how soon one gets really used to that!
Paul: You do get used to it, though. It's really amazing. So that's another cadential possibility. Of course, you can do this *[pointing out on the blackboard],* and you can double this, you can invert the tones, you can have them any way you like. You can have four voices: for instance, you can have this: (27)–(28). Play from here. *[Jean plays the progression (18) through (22) and concludes with (27)–(28).]* . . . Sounds so suitable, doesn't it? Sounds so absolutely right.
Clive: So lawful in itself.
Paul: Yes. I think Yasser did a remarkable thing in working out these cadences.

Now, we can have a progression as a cadence, using the second degree, then going to the fifth, and then going to the first. So this would be two–five–one:

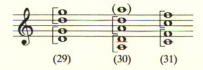

(29)   (30)   (31)

Would you play the chord on the second degree? *[Jean plays the lower dyads at (29)–(30)–(31).]* . . . That's right. All right, now double them. Make them interesting. [Jean repeats, doubling the dyads.] . . . Yes, you can have contrary motion. [The sequence is repeated with the A at (30) tripled.] . . . That's right. Once more. . . .

   Now, you're going to play again from here (18), and this time you'll go from there (22) to this cadence (29)–(30)–(31). . . . Good. Now you play this, and Jane, would you sing freely above it in the scale? Play it just in that tempo from here (18), and from here, to the three-chord cadence. *[As Jean repeats the progression, Jane W. improvises vocally.]* . . . Lovely, very nice. Do it again. *[repetition].* . . . Lovely, very nice. Thank you, Jean.

   So now we have cadences. And when you're doing your exercises, when you're doing your improvisations, use the cadence so you begin to have the feeling of it. *[playing]:*

continued on next page

continued from preceding page

Slower

EXAMPLE 15-1. Improvisation illustrating pentatonic harmonization and cadence.

. . . . It really is beautiful training for the ear, and it's going to make a great deal of difference in the way you use the scale.

You can also have a two-note, naturally, a two-note cadence, if you're improvising with one melody in each hand:

This would be an example of one moving properly, according to harmonic rules in contrary motion.

THREE-TONE "PENTATONIC SEVENTH CHORDS"

Can you take a little more, because I'd like to go further. Let's go to the pentatonic seventh chords. You'll find nice examples—I hope they're nice—in your book *Creative Music Therapy,* *[in the chapter entitled]* Three-Tone Chords.

Merete, will you come to the piano, please? If we start on C and skip D and G, which would be the thing to do in making this chord, wouldn't it—just as you always omit a tone in making chords in the diatonic—you would get this chord. Would you play it, please:

(32)   (33)   (34)   (35)   (36)   (37)   (38)

(32). . . . You can hear that this is unacceptable. You simply couldn't use it. So rather than that, you would use that (33) . . . and that would simply be a doubling of the tonic tone. In other words, you could not have a three-tone chord on the C. Is that clear? But on the D the next tone from G would be the C. . . . That's it, beautiful chord. Go from this one (33) to this one (34). . . . *[Merete alternates the chords.]* . . . Good. Let's take it (34) out and put it here *[writing]*, because later we will be inverting it.

Now, on F, it would be A and D (35). . . . That also doesn't sound right at all, it's quite unacceptable, so that we cannot form a chord on the F, and we do that *[writing (36)]*. Would you play these three now (33)–(34)–(36) . . . and back (34)–(33). . . . Makes a nice progression in itself, doesn't it? On the G—

Elaine: Can you form one on the F—being F, C, and D?
Paul: No, then you'd be skipping two tones, wouldn't you? You'd be skipping the G and the A. It's every other tone that we're omitting. *[proceeding to G]* If we omit the A we get C; if we omit the D we get F (37) . . . this one (34) . . . this one (37) . . . *[Merete plays the indicated chords]* (33) . . . (36) . . . (37) . . . (36) . . . (34) . . . (33). . . .
Paul: And on the A, Merete?
Merete: It would be a C, I think—no, no, no, D, and G.
Paul: —and G (38). So we have one, two, three available seventh chords: (34), (37), and (38). Would you play the three, please? (34) . . . (37) . . . (38). . . . See, they're composed of two fourths, just as our triads are composed of two thirds. But in this scale, the two fourths happen to be not consonant chords, but dissonant chords. And we use them freely, in clinical pentatonic work. Play them all now from the first. . . .
Merete: All of them?
Paul: All of them that are there. (33) . . . (34) . . . (36) . . . (37) . . . (38) . . . and down (37) . . . (36) . . . (34) . . . (33):

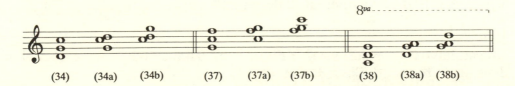

    (34)   (34a)   (34b)   (37)   (37a)   (37b)   (38)   (38a)   (38b)

All right, now let's take this one (34), and invert it; and the first thing we do *[writing]* is put the bottom note an octave higher (34a) . . . that's right. Play this first (34) . . . (34a) . . . And then we put *[the G on top]* (34b). . . . That's it. So those are the three positions possible for each one of these chords. Would you do each one that way, please, Merete?

Merete: The first one?
Paul: The first one. (34) . . . (34a) . . . (34b) . . . (37) . . . (37a) . . . (37b) . . . (38) *[an octave higher]* . . . (38a) . . . (38b). . . . So that gives us a great variety, doesn't it? All right, now let's jump around here a little bit.
Knud: Just a moment. I don't quite understand the upper line there. Why are these called seventh chords, not triads, when you skip every other tone?

Paul: Because the triad in the pentatonic has only two tones. The first
          harmonies we did were the triads, which are called dyads.

I don't want to get too theoretical, but in the pentatonic the possibility for a triad is only a
dyad. And these are the *consonant* chords, so to speak. And what corresponds to our seventh
chord is now this, a three-tone chord. It's all reduced, you see. All right, let's start with this
one *[Merete plays as directed]:* (33) . . . (37) . . . (34b) . . . (34a) . . . (17) . . . (21) . . . (34) . . .
(37) . . . (38) . . . (34a) . . . (17). . . . Good. (21) . . . (20) . . . (38) . . . (22) . . . (25) . . . (24). . . .
Good. That's very rough and haphazard, but it gives you some idea of the kind of harmonic
progression that is possible.

EXERCISES IN PENTATONIC IMPROVISATION

And you will find on one of your pages these chords *[referring to the manuscript in process
of* Creative Music Therapy, *first edition, from which the students are working].* You will find
them used in cadences, and you will also find the dyads, the two-tone chords, with these
three-tone chords—I've made it simple and called them two-tone chords and three-tone
chords rather than dyads and seventh chords because this would be just too confusing.
Maybe you would play this one for us, Merete:

EXAMPLE 15-2. Harmonic progression combining two- and three-tone chords.
Exercise from Nordoff and Robbins, *Creative Music Therapy.*

. . . . Good. Once more, now do it with pedal so that you hold each one. . . . Good. The
dominant begins to sound like a dominant, doesn't it?

Students: Yes, yes.
Paul: Do you have that experience? It really does. Thank you, Merete. It really
          does begin to sound like a dominant.

It is also possible to go further, as you will see on the following page in your book, and have
a four-tone chord on certain notes of the scale; they sound then like this:

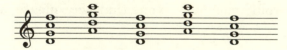

EXAMPLE 15-3. Four-tone chords.

. . . they're composed of really wonderful sounds. . . *[incorporates a cadence].* . . . All right,
Jane Healey, you sing freely now, all right? *[continuing in the general style of the example
with Jane improvising freely with a clear soprano voice].* . . . Good! Lovely. Very nice.

Now, I'll just play you some of the exercises that are here, and these are all examples, these are all just examples for you:

EXAMPLE 15-4. Two-, three-, and four-tone chords.

. . . of three- and four-tone chords (a) . . . *[playing and extending the exercise]* . . . and two-, three-, and four-tones together (b). . . .
Then there are examples of short melodic phrases:

EXAMPLE 15-5. Short melodic phrases with cadence.

You can extend any of these *[demonstrating]* . . . and so on.

OSTINATO ACCOMPANIMENTS

There's an example of a melody with an ostinato accompaniment using the fourth . . . and the seventh:

EXAMPLE 15-6. Melodies with ostinato accompaniment.

(a) . . . *[extending the exercise and varying the ostinato rhythmically].* . . . You can play around with it in that way. And here's an ostinato . . . with an octave, second, fifth (b) . . . *[playing the example as written and extending it; then doubling the ostinato two octaves lower and singing]:* la la-la-la, come on, sing. . . . *[The students join in, each one singing his or her own melodic invention.]* . . . That's nice. Isn't it beautiful? *[The students, excited by their experience, laugh and comment enthusiastically.]*

THE SPECIAL QUALITIES OF THE PENTATONIC

Isn't it beautiful, really beautiful! You have a marvelous scale in which you cannot get a diatonic dissonance. But everything really sounds logical and well, as long as your harmonic accompaniment obeys certain rules—when you sing, or the melody you play, or the number of people who sing—it's all going to combine to make a most beautiful tonal experience. And some children need just that—beautiful tonal experiences. This is what Barton *[see below]* needed, as I said this morning, to be *bathed* in the pentatonic.

Clive: Kind of a cosmos of tone, isn't it?
Paul: Oh, it really is just extraordinary.

TWO-PART MELODIES

Then I've given you some incomplete melodic phrases that you are to go on then and complete yourself.
    An example of a two-part melody:

EXAMPLE 15-7. Incomplete melodic phrases: two-part melody.

. . . . Now if you put that up here *[playing both voices two octaves higher and extending the improvisation]* . . . it's the sort of thing Barton had. It's lovely to become accustomed to playing for a long period of time in an uncomfortable register of the piano, so that you'll be ready to do it if a child needs it.

BARTON, AN ILLUSTRATION OF CLINICAL APPLICATION

[The students had listened to the following case study a few hours earlier.]
    Barton attended a day-care unit for young autistic children. He began music therapy at the age of six. He had no language, and none of his behavior was communicative. He seemed caught up in ritualistic movements, twirling his hands, and running back and forth

repeatedly across a room. He was withdrawn from the adults and children around him in the unit, although he did seem to have developed some degree of closeness and trust with his day-care worker. The clinical team in the unit suspected an organic deficit, which was later confirmed in differential diagnosis. We were impressed by Barton's delicacy, by the lightness and dancelike gracefulness of his movements. He was vulnerable to sense impressions, particularly to loud sounds, and we saw much of his autistic behavior to be a shrinking away from a world he found incomprehensible and oppressive. There were several instances when the loud recordings of children's songs and ring-games the day-care staff used in their group sessions—together with the singing of a group of enthusiastic adults—obviously overwhelmed him, and he appeared stunned and distressed in these sessions.

In an early music therapy session, he was observed by Dr. Herbert Geuter, then a consultant to the project. *[For information on the part played by Dr. Geuter in the development of the Nordoff-Robbins approach to music therapy, see* Therapy in Music for Handicapped Children.*]* He recommended the use of pentatonic improvisations in a high register, and that we record a commentary on the sessions, closely observing Barton's movements.

Initially, all his music was improvised in the high treble of the piano, and consisted mostly of two-part melodies *[as in Example 15-7]*. Other styles of playing were introduced freely: using progressions and cadences, *[as in Examples 15-1 to 15-5]*, ostinatos *[as in Example 15-6]*, and gamelanlike improvisations *[see Examples 15-8 and 15-9 below]*. The bright, ringing tones of this music, coupled with its openness and rhythmic energy, created a refreshing, invigorating environment to which Barton responded positively. After a brief period of acclimation, he consistently showed his delight in the music, frequently smiling and laughing. His pleasure was also expressed in his animated movements, which increasingly reflected the rhythm of the music as he danced and stepped, clearly in response to the tempos and phrasings of the improvisations.

One of his habitual postures was to walk about with his thumbs pressed into his neck immediately below his ears; his index, middle, and fourth fingers curled over; and his little fingers extended out sideways, flicking in and out. We noticed that soon the little fingers were flicking in time to the music. Everything about him was delicately alive and mobile. Spontaneously, he invented little structured dance patterns for himself, or his arms moved in a half-spiral across his body, one arm taking up the movement where the other left off. He was sensitive to changes of tempo, melodic character, and register. We added a cluster of small Asian bells, which he would move with his feet as he danced or ran; a cymbal; and bongos—which, to his fascination, the cotherapist played lightly. There was a synergy in the way the three of us interrelated in the music, and in the way his feeling life absorbed and resonated to the pentatonic. Session by session, he took the initiative to approach us, and tentatively at first, then purposefully, begin to participate in our playing. In his later sessions, he began to sing phrases and held tones with us; we were aware that his singing was self-expressive.

The sessions lasted between fifteen and twenty-five minutes. At the closure of every session, the transition from the special world of his music to the environment of the day-care milieu was made through *Goodbye! [Example 1-12]* with its diatonic harmony and primally simple melody. Gradually, during the eighteen sessions we shared, the therapist introduced diatonic harmonies into the improvisations, particularly dissonances in a high register. This was done as Barton's self-confidence, and his security in our music-sharing relationship, continued to grow. In this way musical tensions were brought into the sessions that were more in affinity with the music he was normally exposed to, tensions which were more directly expressive of the drives and demands of everyday external life. His acceptance was positive.

ASPECTS OF A JAVANESE GAMELAN STYLE

I think I'll tell you this story—we have time. Clive and I were in Rotterdam in 1960, and we were to get a freighter for New York, and the freighter was delayed a day—you know, you're never sure when a freighter's going to sail. So we wandered around and we went into the— what was the name of the museum?

[It was The Ethnological Museum, where we found a collection of Indonesian instruments on display. Paul asked the attendant if they had a gamelan. This led to a meeting with the museum's curator, who was immediately interested when we explained that we were music therapists and that we often used pentatonic improvisation in Chinese and Indonesian styles in our work with developmentally disabled children. He led us into a side hall—it was not part of the exhibit—drew a curtain, and there was a complete Javanese gamelan! This was an exciting surprise, but more was to come: to our delight, we were invited to join a small ensemble of museum staff in playing the gamelan. Paul was assigned to four gongs, one of them large and heavy, with a wonderfully deep sonority. I was given a bonnang to play—a gong chime of ten pitched gongs resting on cords in a wooden frame. We played in a pentatonic scale: E, F♯, A, B, C♯, and mostly in the first mode. There were charted scores to guide us. The curator first demonstrated the instruments and taught us different ostinatos. Then, sitting in the "lotus position" with a drum before him, he led us into a succession of fascinating experiences of this idiom and this style of playing.]

Oh, he was simply wonderful, and he led us so beautifully and through wonderful changes of tempo. This is what I'm going to see if we can approximate somehow tomorrow in our group work. And this is an attempt to duplicate . . . the sound of that very big gong:

EXAMPLE 15-8. Illustrating a gong effect in a gamelan-style improvisation.

. . . . The tempo would change like this . . . it was simply wonderful. And then the ritards never stopped.

Clive: You couldn't believe a ritard could be that slow.
Paul: You couldn't *believe* a ritard could last so long and be so slow. If you were:

EXAMPLE 15-9. Illustrating an extended ritard in gamelan style.

Clive: It's only halfway there.

. . . *[continuing the ritard and concluding the improvisation].* . . . It's a fantastic musical experience, really! And how he conducted this with his drum. It was a wonderful experience. And this was just on the eve of our going to America, and then we find Barton, and Dr. Geuter says "use the pentatonic." You know this was still in our ears.

PENTATONIC VERSUS DIATONIC HARMONIZATION

[After more discussion of traditional Indonesian music, the exploration turned again to considering the lightening and releasing effect of the pentatonic, its openness, and its freedom from the necessities and densities of conventional diatonic harmonization.]
You know, the Native Americans have beautiful pentatonic folk songs—and they are usually harmonized with diatonic harmony. So you have something that goes:

EXAMPLE 15-10. A Native American melody and a conventional harmonization.

[Playing and singing the melody alone] . . . and you find it's harmonized: *[playing the four measures with accompaniment. The students laugh at the lush arpeggiated diatonic accompaniment.]* Really, truly! It happens all the time.
And there's a very ancient and beautiful Chinese melody that goes:

continued on next page

continued from preceding page

(39)

EXAMPLE 15-11. An ancient Chinese melody with Western and pentatonic harmonizations.

[Playing the melody only, an octave lower than written]. . . . Isn't that nice! Now in the nineteenth century, a famous German scholar harmonized it like this *[playing the complete diatonic arrangement,[1] up to the double bar].* . . . *[The students are amused by the romantic Western patterns of harmony and accompaniment.]* Now, Mr. Yasser proves his beautiful harmonization, and the justification of it: *[plays the second harmonization]* . . . hear the dominant (39) . . . ? So much more fitting, and so much truer, isn't it? Really beautiful.

A STUDENT PRESENTS A CHINESE FOLK SONG

Unni says she has a Chinese melody she'd like to sing for us. Will you, Unni?

Unni: Yes. It's a little melody that I learned when I used to live with a Chinese family. Will you play chords underneath, Paul?

Paul: Yes.

Unni: And it's a short song that the father of the family does as a lullaby for the little daughter. And her name was "Shalwang." Actually it was Leanne, but her nickname was "Shalwang," which means "little flower." And the English translation is:

> Hello, hello to you green acres
> That house the heart of little flower
> So that it can bloom freely when it is ripe
> And fly across you with butterfly wings
> But always return.

Paul: Ah. Lovely. I'll play just where you want.

Unni: You just play—anything:

---

[1] A.W. Ambros, *Geschichte der Musik*, Breslau, 1862.

EXAMPLE 15-12. *Shalwang's Lullaby*, Chinese folk song, sung by Unni Johns with improvised accompaniment.

. . . . [The song is in the second mode on D.] . . . Beautiful! [acclaim from the students]

Clive: Encore!

Paul: You have to do it again. Really beautiful. *[repeating the words]* Let's
do this again. *[The song is repeated.]* . . . Well, you made us a beautiful
present. Thank you. Just lovely. Would you make me a copy of that?

Unni: Yes.

Paul: I'd love to have it. I think that's a lovely note on which to finish the day.

EDITOR'S
NOTE
    The discussions and illustrations in this exploration that demonstrate the inappropriateness of certain traditional pentatonic melodies being harmonized diatonically were not intended to imply that all pentatonic melodies should be harmonized pentatonically. There are many predominantly pentatonic melodies in folk music and the popular repertoire that are unmistakably diatonic in character and obviously require diatonic harmonization. Many are of Western origin: Appalachian, Irish, and Scottish folk songs present many such melodies; even where the accompaniment is as simple as a drone bass this is clearly diatonic as it consists of the tonic and dominant of the "home" diatonic key. Such melodies often contain one or more diatonic passing tones. They are usually in the third mode of the pentatonic, the mode that has closest affinity with the diatonic major scale. In clinical work there are many striking instances of diatonically harmonized pentatonic melodies being used effectively; To Make Some Music, a third-mode melody, and Goodbye! (page 12 of this book), the melody of which uses four tones of a first mode pentatonic, were of great importance in Anna's course of therapy. See P. Nordoff and C. Robbins, Creative Music Therapy (New York: John Day, 1977).

EXPLORATION SIXTEEN
TONAL RELATIONSHIPS THAT LINK
ARCHETYPAL SCALE FORMS

*B*uilding a pentatonic scale using five consecutive tones from the circle of fifths. Adding the sixth and seventh tones from the circle of fifths to form a diatonic scale (in the Lydian mode); using these as passing tones in the pentatonic to create a state of transition from one archetypal scale to another. Bringing the tritone, the major seventh, and the minor second—the intervals of greatest tension—into the scale by changing any tone that alters the fundamental form of the pentatonic. The powerful effects of the distinctly different mood this creates. Changing two tones in the pentatonic to produce an archaic Greek scale, which is also a Japanese scale in current use. Adding the two "missing" (diatonic) tones to pentatonic and altered pentatonic scales to create the diatonic modes. Changing tones in the modes to create Middle Eastern scales.

IMPROVISING IN THE PENTATONIC WITH DIATONIC PASSING TONES

We're going to have some interesting ideas this afternoon about passing from one archetype to another. We've gone from the children's tune to the pentatonic, and now we will go from the pentatonic to altered pentatonics, which lead us directly into modes.

Amanda, would you help us in our research today? Let's use these two-tone chords *[dyads]* of the pentatonic and improvise freely—perhaps in that rhythm.

Use this as an ostinato. And just play the scale freely above it. All right? Can you see it?

Amanda: Yes.

EXAMPLE 16-1. *Student improvisation in the pentatonic using an ostinato comprising dyads.*

. . . . Oh, isn't it nice to hear it again! An old friend. . . . Lovely.

Now just think—remember the old circle of fifths that you're taught in school to learn the number of flats and sharps? Well, Mr. Yasser, quite rightly, begins his circle of fifths with F. And so it would go like this, wouldn't it:

F–C–G–D–A

And there are the five tones of the scale you're using. Right? And the next fifth from A would be?

Students: E.
Paul: And the one above that would be?
Students: B.
Paul: This would be E and this would be B. Quite right. And those are the two
          tones that are missing here.

F–C–G–D–A	E–B
pentatonic scale	missing tones

Now, Amanda, could you do something very interesting? Use E and B as passing tones in your improvisation against this *[first mode pentatonic on F]*, and I mean really as passing tones, never on the beat. So you would, for instance, go *[singing]*:

p = passing tone

. . . never hitting them on the beat, never giving them anything more than the importance of a passing tone.

Amanda: Giving them only the importance of passing between two others?
Paul: Between the two tones they are between, they're only passing tones.
Amanda: Is that the only way to use them? Can you go to one of them and back
        again to the same tone?
Paul: Yes, you can do that.

EXAMPLE 16-2. Student improvisation in the pentatonic, with diatonic passing tones.

. . . . Good. Do you feel it loses its pentatonic character?

Students: Oh, yes!

It's already on its way somewhere else, isn't it? And it's very interesting to read in Mr. Yasser's book that actually there was a time in China, I don't know how long it lasted, when these two notes were taken into the scale, and for a time they had a seven-tone scale. But it was found very uncongenial, and it was soon given up. It was never done in sacred music, naturally. This only happened in folk music—and only in certain parts of China, too, I believe, as well. But the moment one does do that, the true pentatonic character is lost and one is really in a kind of transitional stage between one archetypal scale and another. Thank you, Amanda.

ALTERED PENTATONICS AND THEIR CLINICAL EFFECTS

Now, I do want you to copy this because these are altered pentatonic scales that have some importance. You may never use them, and then again, you may want to use one for, I should say, a fairly young, deeply emotionally disturbed child.

I have only once used one—I think I've used one since[1]—but once with a tremendous, unexpected effect, and that is with the very first child Dr. Geuter asked me to work with at Sunfield. Johnny wandered around the room; he did come to the piano and play a strange rhythm several times with one hand, a cluster played rapidly twice, the first time as an accented sixteenth note—a little bit like Andrew's triplet *[Andrew was a child currently in music therapy]* except it was a sixteenth note, actually, but that much quicker. But when I began to play in one of these altered pentatonic scales, Johnny began to cry, very seriously cry. He didn't like it—well, I don't know whether he liked it or not—but he cried. I changed and went back to a normal pentatonic, and he stopped crying. Then I improvised, I think, in a mode, and so forth, and I thought, "Well, I wonder if this would provoke the same response." So I went back to that altered pentatonic and he cried again.[2] Which is really a very curious thing and led to the first big question in my mind—in working with an individual child—what is a tonal experience? And what is the emotional effect of different kinds of tone on a child?

ALTERING THE PENTATONIC TO INTRODUCE TENSION

So let me just give you these, but first of all—Jane Healey, would you help me this time. Let's take this scale. Would you play it for us:

(a).... Good. Now, would you lower one of the tones of the scale, let's say the second tone of the scale: (b)... and down please.... The moment we do that we have what in the way of interval experience that we haven't had in the normal pentatonic?

Students: Semitone, major sevenths—
Paul: We have everything that we hadn't had before. We have the tritone E♭–A, we have the minor second, right here *[D–E♭]*, and we have the possibility from the E♭ to the D, of the major seventh.

So, all the tensions that exist in the present diatonic scale are there immediately when you alter a tone of the pentatonic. *[There are only two exceptions: taking the group of three consecutive tones, the lower tone may be flatted by a semitone, or the upper tone raised by a semitone, without losing a normal pentatonic scale configuration. In each change you move into another mode.]* I think that's a very interesting thing. Would you play it for us again, please, Jane.... Now using these intervals as an ostinato in three:

---

[1] See the use of the children's tune in E minor with Pernilla in P. Nordoff and C. Robbins, *Creative Music Therapy* (New York: John Day, 1977), Band 67.
[2] See P. Nordoff and C. Robbins, *Therapy in Music for Handicapped Children* (London: Victor Gollancz, 1992), p. 28.

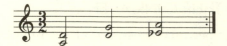

Improvise, then, with these notes above, all right?

EXAMPLE 16-3. Student improvisation in an altered pentatonic, with one altered tone.

. . . [After a strong beginning, Jane becomes momentarily confused.] . . .

Jane: Sorry.

. . . . Threw you out. You were doing beautifully until you made that mistake . . . play it firmly. *. . . . [Jane continues successfully.] . . .*

CHANGING TWO TONES CREATES A POWERFUL CHANGE OF MOOD

All right, now this . . . let's do this. Play the scale first:

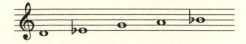

. . . and down. *. . . .* Play the original scale *[D–E–G–A–B]. . . .* Always firmly. Now the first alteration with E♭ and B♮ . . . and down. *. . . .* Now with the second alteration *[E♭ and B♭]. . . .* Good! Now with the ostinato:

EXAMPLE 16-4. Student improvisation in an altered pentatonic, with two altered tones.

. . . . Good. All right? Thank you. Elaine, how do you like the sound of this?

Students: Very sad.
Nancy: It's Japanese, isn't it, Paul?
Paul: This is an archaic Greek scale! Isn't that an interesting thing? *[Asiatic influence is evident in some surviving fragments of early Greek music.]*

Elaine, would you come to the piano, please?

Now we're using the dominant—that's the dominant (1)—we're using the dominant here . . . instead of here (2).

Elaine: Do you want me to use that scale?
Paul: Play this ostinato and use the same scale:

continued on next page

continued from preceding page

EXAMPLE 16-5. Student improvisation in an altered pentatonic, with two altered tones and a different ostinato.

. . . . Good.

MOVING FROM ALTERED PENTATONICS INTO THE DIATONIC MODES

Now if you play this in the scale:

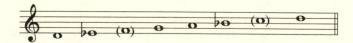

EXAMPLE 16-6. Altered pentatonic scale leading to the Phrygian mode.

. . . the two missing tones in the scale. . . . Which mode do we have?

Unni: Phrygian.
Paul: The Phrygian mode. Isn't that fascinating?

So that already, as I said, in the altered pentatonics, we are approaching the Greek modes. When the two missing tones, which could be used as passing tones in this altered pentatonic, are brought into the scale, we then find the Phrygian. Thank you, Elaine, that was a nice one.

Merete, let us take this mode:

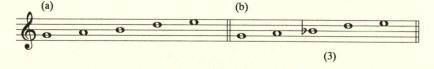

Just play it naturally first (a). . . . Now with a B♭ (b). . . .

I would like to just point out that this, in the *[altered]* pentatonic, the B♭–D, is equivalent in the diatonic to the step and a half. You can grasp that immediately, can't you? That enormous change here *[from B to B♭],* which widens this interval (3), is the equivalent in the diatonic to *[singing a phrase in a Middle Eastern scale]:*

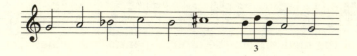

. . . and here *[singing a similar phrase in an altered pentatonic]:*

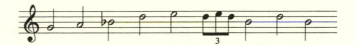

One has the same feeling exactly within the pentatonic as one has in the diatonic with the step and a half. Would you play this now with the second alteration:

. . . yes, and now, for an ostinato, let us use—we can't use the B♭, we have to use the fifth— let's use all fifths, all inverted fourths, as an ostinato in three:

. . . . *[Merete plays the ostinato but has difficulty sustaining a melody over it.]*

Merete: Ah, I'm sorry. . . . It's really very hard to do.
Paul: You find that difficult?
Merete: Yes.
Paul: Good! Well, practice that one then, would you? Good.
Merete: Now?—not now!
Paul: Not now.

This is a Japanese one, Nancy—*[singing in the above scale]*—a Japanese one that is still being used today, although it's very, very old. It's very interesting, we saw a Japanese film some time ago, and the music was still based in this scale.

Now if we add again the missing tones, play the seven-tone scale, we have now:

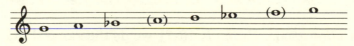

EXAMPLE 16-7. Altered pentatonic scale leading to the Aeolian mode.

. . . . And which mode was that?

Students: Aeolian.
Paul: Aeolian, right?

You could build all of the modes from the altered pentatonic scales. You take this one:

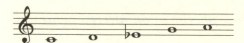

You add an F and a B♭—somebody come and play this, please. Jean. Just play the pentatonic first . . . and now bring the other two notes in:

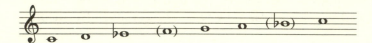

EXAMPLE 16-8. Altered pentatonic scale leading to the Dorian mode.

. . . . And what mode do we have?

Jane H.:   The Dorian.
Paul: You have the Dorian mode.

MOVING FROM THE MODES INTO MIDDLE EASTERN SCALES

Let's do something really fantastic and interesting, and we will do that [raising the fourth tone]:

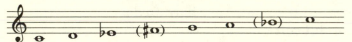

EXAMPLE 16-9. Altered pentatonic scale leading to a Middle Eastern scale.

. . . and down . . . and we have a Middle Eastern scale. We can alter tones of these modes to find our Middle Eastern scales. With the Phrygian [Example 16-6], if we raise the F to F♯ and the C to C♯ we get another Middle Eastern scale. Would you play that for us:

EXAMPLE 16-10. Altering the Phrygian mode to produce a second Middle Eastern scale.

. . . . And here [the Aeolian mode, Example 16-7], we do the same thing [raising the C to C♯ and the F to F♯]:

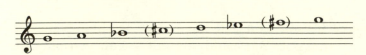

EXAMPLE 16-11. Altering the Aeolian mode to produce a third Middle Eastern scale.

Jean: *[after some confusion over the placement of the step and a half]* I was
            thinking about the first one.
Paul: You don't have a step and a half there *[Example 16-7]*. But here
            [Example 16-11], between six and seven you do.
Jean: Yes, I didn't realize there were different scales. I thought there was only
            one Middle Eastern scale.
Paul: Play it. Play this one *[Example 16-9]*. . . . And play this one *[Example
            16-11]*. . . .

The first part of the scale is the same, but the last part of the scale is quite different. But
don't you think it is interesting that this can be done—was done—in the travels from East
to West, from the Far East to the Middle East to the Mediterranean—the Greeks had five-
tone scales, too, you see, before the seven-tone evolved. And the famous modal scales we
know as "Greek," with little alteration, suit the climate, the personality, the temperament of
the people in Turkey, in Syria, and in all the Middle Eastern countries, where you feel the
modes would not be correct. This step and a half is absolutely essential for the expression of
these people.

Amanda: It does make our diatonic system seem, in a way, kind of contrived,
          beyond something archetypal, beyond something natural.
Paul: No, the great archetype in our system is, of course, what developed from
          the seven tones, when the octave, when the twelve tones were found
          capable of being divided within an octave *[in the tempering of the tones]*
          and one could move from key to key. This is an enrichment of the
          archetype. This was there all the time, and our music is inconceivable
          without it.

So, what I'm going to do now is to write out another Middle Eastern scale with a suggested
bass. And then you can improvise freely with the scales above.

EXAMPLE 16-12. Middle Eastern scale with suggested ostinato bass.

Now, who is the brave person who will have a go at this? Nancy. Try the ostinato first.
Daaaaa bom-bom . . . that's it. You could, actually—can you play the C and D with your
thumb?

Nancy: Yes . . . it's gymnastics!
Paul: You don't have to hold the G, but it's a nice idea to.
Nancy: No, but it's nice.
Paul: All right, hold it. *[singing with Nancy's ostinato]:*

. . . you might want to play something?

EXAMPLE 16-13. Student improvisation in a Middle Eastern scale; Nordoff and then the class sing freely.

. . . . Don't let your dynamics drop . . . *[beating out the rhythm and singing]* . . . keep them going. . . . Yes, get the feeling, don't phrase it, don't get soft *[singing]*. . . . Come on, sing, somebody. *[The students join in singing.]* Stimulating, isn't it? *[laughter]* Thank you.

Now you can do that same base, holding the G, Nancy, which is a very nice thing to do. Hold it through. *[Nancy playing]*. . . . Yes, good! In that case, you would have to write it like this *[as in Example 16-6]*. And if you finger this with your thumb, it's much easier to do.

Alfred: Paul!
Paul: Yes.
Alfred: May I suggest that when improvising, a melody shouldn't necessarily start on the beat?
Paul: Start off the beat; and don't start with scale steps. I mean, certainly use scale steps, but remember always that melodies are always composed of skips and scale tones, and that one of the most typical things in Middle Eastern music is the wavering back and forth between this interval *[singing to demonstrate]* . . . this kind of thing, between that one and a half steps. The F♯–E♭.
Elaine: Quite a different experience singing this to singing pentatonic.
Paul: Absolutely different, isn't it? And the whole feeling is different. It's hot! You know? It's got—it's not just warm—this really has a hot kind of intensity.
Clive: Dry.
Paul: You can see where it belongs to hot, dry countries. Absolutely right!
Clive: There's no twilight. Daylight—night.
Jane H.: It's rather sinuous as well.
Paul: Oh, yes, of course, it has all that, naturally. If you've ever seen any good belly dancing, you've heard music like this.

EDITOR'S   *At the time these explorations were made, virtually the only Arabian music heard in the West, other*
NOTE   *than performances by specialist groups or in university departments of ethnomusicology, originat-*
            ed in restaurants offering Middle Eastern cuisine and featuring female dancers performing what
            was popularly known as belly dancing. Since then, immigrant Islamic communities have developed
            in many urban centers, and a wider variety of Arabian music is becoming known. Paul Nordoff
            explored quite different moods and styles of music based on Middle Eastern scales, often with strik-
            ing clinical effect. Obviously, it was not possible to make the piano replicate the timbres and pitch-
            es produced by an authentic regional ensemble, but that was not his intention. What he strove to
            achieve in the therapy situation was a specialized piano and vocal interpretation of the expressive
            character of the idiom. He based his improvisations on the stability of the tetrachords (1–4, 5–8)
            common to the structures of diatonic and much Middle Eastern music, and frequently used his voice
            to achieve the subtle shadings of tone and mood associated with the scale(s). In situations that
            called for heightened stimulation, he also used the piano to add the effect of rhythmically impelling
            accompanying percussion.[3]

[3] Refer to the audio recordings of Anna in P. Nordoff and C. Robbins, *Creative Music Therapy* (New York: John Day, 1977), Bands 17, 18, 21, 24, 26, and 27.

EXPLORATION SEVENTEEN
INTRODUCTION TO THE SPANISH IDIOM

Links between Spanish music and organum: the extensive use of fifths in the accompaniment, and parallel motion in chords, both characteristic of the folk music of Spain and the piano literature in Spanish style. The influence both of the music of the Catholic church, and of the Arabian styles and scales of the Moorish conquerors, on Spanish music. The habanera, or tango, rhythm as further evidence of the Middle Eastern influence. The dance-song-dance form, a manifestation of the A-B-A archetype; the cante hondo or deep song; and a harmonic ambivalence of major and minor. Examples of the Spanish music of Lecuona, Ravel, Falla, and Debussy. Compositions by Joaquin Nin-Culmell in various regional Spanish styles: improvisational resources in a variety of metrical and rhythmic dance forms.

SIMILARITIES BETWEEN ORGANUM AND THE SPANISH IDIOM

When we come to the idiom I want us to be working on this week, we find an interesting parallel to what we have in the organum chords:

continued on next page

continued from preceding page

(2)

EXAMPLE 17-1a. Lecuona, *Malagueña*, opening.

. . . . *[(1) The fifths in the bass are briefly demonstrated in their rhythm.]* . . . Left hand *[continuing to (2)].* . . .

Students: Olé!
Paul: Olé! What is the similarity we have? First of all, we have the fifth, which you will find in much Spanish music. What else do we have? A certain way of composing music—how are these chords moving?
Amanda: Parallel.
Paul: Parallel motion. You get parallel motion in Spanish music. These marvelous links between the musical culture of one country and another.

THE ARABIAN INFLUENCE AND THE DANCE-SONG-DANCE FORM

You must also not forget that the Arabs—the "Moors"—conquered Spain and lived there for a long time, and so Arabian music influenced Spanish music. One hears that still today in much of the folk music of Spain.

   Now we have an interesting new archetype. Or rather, it is not a new archetype, but a manifestation of it, an interpretation of it. And that is that we have in an important part of Spain, Andalusia: dance, followed by song, followed by dance. And this gives us what musical form?

Jane H.:   A-B-A?

Paul: The A-B-A. That is the archetype, isn't it? The musical forms are naturally archetypes.

If you look at the Spanish music composed by Ravel, by Debussy, by Lecuona, by Falla, you will find this dance-song-dance idea is absolutely the form of the piece. In this *Malagueña* that I just began to play for you, when the dance finishes *[recommencing playing in measure 55]*:

continued on next page

EXAMPLE 17-1b. Lecuona, *Malagueña*, song section.

. . . ending the first part. . . . Now comes the song . . . that's the strumming of the guitar (3) . . . *[continuing through the song]* . . . and the dance takes on again.

THE CANTE HONDO

This is marvelous form, and the song part of this particular kind of dance is called the cante hondo—deep song. The men mostly sing it, and they have the most beautiful coloratura facility in the use of their voices. You find this in that wonderful composition of Ravel—which you should look at some day, *Alborada del Gracioso*, "The Dance of the Court Jester." And Ravel, being the genius he was, naturally transformed the whole of it:

EXAMPLE 17-2a. Ravel, *Alborada del Gracioso* from *Miroirs*, opening.

. . . (4) marvelous chords . . . *[fade at (5)]*. When the first part ends he does the same kind of thing in the middle part, this wonderful singing, the single line to represent the cante hondo:

EXAMPLE 17-2b. Ravel, *Alborada del Gracioso* from *Miroirs*, cante hondo. (Not illustrated on the recording.)

It's really very beautiful, very exciting. So that's one important one.
    Falla has some wonderful things, also.

EXAMPLE 17-3. Falla, *Dance of Terror* from *El Amor Brujo*.

. . . [playing in the style of the composition] . . . I don't remember it all . . . but there again . . . fifths in the accompaniment.

THE ORIGIN OF THE HABANERA RHYTHM

I'll give you a few examples of Spanish harmony, which is a curious mixture of major and minor. Before we go on to that, we mustn't forget this rhythm:

. . . which is the tango rhythm—the habanera rhythm—and which is originally also a Middle Eastern rhythm. It was not discovered in South America—just that someone made a great hit with it there—and it came back to the United States and Europe by way of South America. You pick it up even in Greece today, in some folk music. Greece has Middle Eastern scales from Turkey, and from all of that section. You can still find this habanera rhythm in Greek folk music.

Some beautiful music has been written on that rhythm by Debussy: "The Night in Granada," *La Soirée dans Granade,* which is a beautiful one. Also one in the volume of preludes—the second volume, I think.

Jenny: *La Puerta del Vino.*
Paul: *La Puerta del Vino!* That's right. It's so wonderful that in the *Soirée*—
          in the "Night in Granada"—Debussy so subtly, and delicately, and
          beautifully keeps the feeling of the Middle Eastern influence. After all
          this wonderful:

Mouvement de Habanera

Commencer lentement dans un rythme nonchalamment gracieux

continued on next page

continued from preceding page

(8)

EXAMPLE 17-4. Debussy, *La Soirée dans Granade* from *Estampes*, opening.

. . . again, the dominant and the tonic creating the mood *[the first four measures]* . . . *[continues into the* Tempo giusto*]* . . . then the dominant sevenths (6), (7) . . . parallel motion . . . *[continues to (8)]*.

Don't be afraid of your fifths. Don't be afraid to use the fifth in this particular idiom. And the *Puerta del Vino* starts with fifths, doesn't it:

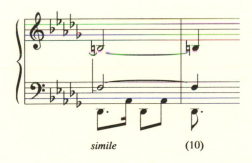

EXAMPLE 17-5. Debussy, *Prelude*, Book 2, no. 3, *La Puerta del Vino*, opening.

. . . *[beginning with the left hand at (9), then stopping at (10)]*. . . . Wonderful what a fifth can do! It sets a stage, sets a mood.

NIN-CULMELL'S COMPOSITIONS IN SPANISH REGIONAL STYLES

Now I have some music of my friend Joaquin Nin-Culmell—some of you know it—just to show you some rhythms, and how beautifully he uses them. First of all, every part of Spain has its own kind of music. Besides this wonderful musical influence by the Moors, there was—going alongside of this—the music in the churches. This is a completely different thing, which is influenced by the music used in the Catholic church all throughout Europe in the tenth, eleventh, and twelfth centuries.

Here's what Joaquin Nin-Culmell does with a dance in 6/8 that comes from the Asturias:

EXAMPLE 17-6. Nin-Culmell, *Copla Asturiana* from *Tonadas*, Vol. 3, no. 26.

. . . . Marvelous rhythm!

Beautiful rhythm!

Here's a very nice one in 2/4:

EXAMPLE 17-7. Nin-Culmell, *Pandeirada* from *Tonadas*, Vol. 3, no. 29.

. . . . Notice again the use of the fifth *[particularly in the left hand on the first beat of alternating measures of the accompaniment].*

Here's a beautiful one alternating 3/8, 4/8:

EXAMPLE 17-8. Nin-Culmell, *Motivo de Santo Domingo,* from *Tonadas*, Vol. 3, no. 30.

. . . . They're very nice.

Nancy: Who are these by?
Paul: Nin-Culmell, the son of Joaquin Nin, who was a minor composer. He's a
           university professor at Berkeley, California. Gives you some nice
           rhythmic ideas:

EXAMPLE 17-9. Nin-Culmell, *Ball pla i L'esquerrana* from *Tonadas*, Vol. 4, no. 42.

. . . that's so typical of the Spanish *[repeating the triplet figures]*, you know that. . . . Those
turns you would certainly use if you were improvising in that idiom.
       This is a nice one:

EXAMPLE 17-10. Nin-Culmell, *Canción de Labrador* from *Tonadas*, Vol. 1, no. 3.

. . . . That's a very lovely one. There again, you have the minor-major ambivalence almost, which is so expressive and so typical of this music.

Sybil: Are they still in print?

Paul: Yes. They're published in New York, and I'm sure they could be ordered. They are a fascinating group of pieces.

Joaquin is a very close friend of Mompou, and sees him every summer when he goes back to Barcelona, where he was born.

EDITOR'S   *The exploration concluded with a demonstration of passages from Fantasia Baetica by Falla,*
NOTE   *"Baetica" being an early Latin name for a region of Spain. This virtuoso piece was presented as Falla's monumental attempt to put the feeling of a whole province of Spain into piano form, and to give an idea of what a Spanish composer could do with his own native materials. The passages played reiterated several of the elements already discussed: the use of the fifth; the imitation of flamenco guitar style; the archetypal dance-song-dance form contrasting impassioned dance rhythms with the cante hondo; melodic ornamentation; and the characteristic combining of major and minor. Although the composition is extremely difficult to play, seldom performed, and at times seems to attempt to capture and express more than the piano can really do, it was recommended as well worth listening to.*

EXPLORATION EIGHTEEN

A REVIEW OF MAJOR AND MINOR THIRDS, LEADING TO AN INTRODUCTION TO ROMANTIC MUSIC

An exploration of melodic and harmonic major and minor thirds in musical archetypes—including pentatonics and their alterations, modes and their alterations, and Middle Eastern scales. The superimposition of thirds as the basis of harmonic construction in Western music. Major and minor harmonies and their emotional impact. Finding the right chord when harmonizing music for therapy. The power of the triad. Singing nonchordal tones in the romantic style; developing the harmony. The tenderness of romantic music and its potential significance in therapy. The importance of the song literature; composers and the poets whose works they choose to set. Schubert's songs and a personal anecdote giving insight into a cultural bias. An experience of romantic harmonization in a Fauré song.

MINOR AND MAJOR THIRDS IN THE PENTATONIC

We want today to think about major and minor thirds. You remember—to go all the way back to our first archetype, the children's tune:

(a)   (b)   (c)

[singing (a)]. . . . Sing it. *[The class sings (a).]* . . . How another one *[a fourth above]* completes the pentatonic scale *[singing (b)].* . . . Sing it. *[The class sings (b).]* . . . *[dividing the class]* This half sing that (b), and this half sing (a) la la-la la la. Ready! *[The class sings (c).]* . . . Isn't that beautiful? Do it again. *[The class repeats (c).]* . . . And the fourth is the interval with which we harmonize our pentatonic:

EXAMPLE 18-1. Improvisation in a pentatonic scale.

. . . . All right, sing freely. *[The students sing freely, closing on a held chord.]*

Beautiful! Isn't that beautiful! And you think of bringing this beautiful scale, these beautiful harmonies, to the children. And we have what kind of thirds?

Students: Minor.

Paul: Minor thirds. But they are used only melodically. They are not used in
          pentatonic harmonization. Then we studied the chromatic alteration of
          the pentatonic, and what happens then? What kind of thirds do we have?

Jane H.: Major.

Paul: We have major thirds with the altered pentatonics, but again, they are
          only used melodically:

continued on next page

continued from preceding page

EXAMPLE 18-2. Improvisation in an altered pentatonic scale.

. . . . Sing freely. *[The class sings freely in the scale.]* . . . Beautiful, beautiful, beautiful! Oh, you're getting to be so good.

So we have, melodically, minor thirds and major thirds appearing. And this is still, you remember, a scale that you find in Japanese music today—much Japanese music today that hasn't been influenced by Western music.

Then when we moved into the modal scales, we found that in the alteration of those, we again discovered:

. . . *[altering the Aeolian mode on G to form a Middle Eastern scale; see Example 16-11, page 176]*, for instance here (1), and in here (2), in the Middle Eastern scale, we again discovered the minor third, right? And in this scale again, the minor third is a melodic experience rather than a harmonic experience in this music:

EXAMPLE 18-3. Improvisation in a Middle Eastern scale.

. . . right! *[The students join in, singing freely in the scale.]* . . . Great!

There again, the real expression of this beautiful idiom lies in just those thirds, those minor thirds. And we all agreed that the scale expressed the heat, the dryness, the poverty, the loneliness, the suffering—it comes out of the folk soul of the people.

This *[the pentatonic]* became, in China, a very sophisticated musical system. It was quite a different thing, which was expressive—oh, in a way that we really cannot grasp, except emotionally—it's very hard to intellectualize it. But here again, one feels that in this alteration of the pentatonic, there was a need to express something very important in the souls, the psyches, of the people for whom this became a natural idiom.

THIRDS AS THE FOUNDATION OF WESTERN HARMONIC CONSTRUCTION

And then we come into Western music and find that these expressive intervals are the basis of an entire system, of a system of music without which we would have no Mozart, no Beethoven. And we came then, very early last term, to our discussion of the intervals. You remember that the thirds—this is Rudolf Steiner's beautiful concept of the inner experience of the intervals—the major and minor third provide an inner experience of balance: balance within oneself; of oneself in one's inner emotional life. The satisfaction that the people must have when they sing this *[indicating major and minor thirds]*. This beautiful inner experience brings a satisfaction and self-realization.

And so through these thirds, by superimposing one on top of another, we have the basis of our whole Western harmonic system. And we go on adding to make sevenths, ninths, elevenths, and thirteenth chords. In the course of time, all of these have been taken into music, and in the twentieth century now we have these used so much and so beautifully and expressively by Ravel.

THE FALLACY OF CONSIDERING MAJOR AS HAPPY AND MINOR AS SAD

How important it is, in a composition we hear by one of our great composers, whether it is in a minor or in a major key. And yet, wouldn't it be ridiculous to stop at the usual conception that minor is sad and major is happy? The saddest songs in the world:

EXAMPLE 18-4. Foster, *The Old Folks at Home.*

. . . are in major. *Old Black Joe*—and *Believe Me, If All Those Endearing Young Charms*— all these heartbreakers are in the major scale.

SUDDEN, EXPRESSIVE SHIFTS BETWEEN MAJOR AND MINOR

In the Spanish idiom, we talked about the beautiful shift—the sudden shift—between major and minor. How in the major sequence of chords there will be one minor one, like the flick of the lizard's tongue, you know, on a hot rock in the south of Spain. And how, in the romantic idiom we're going to be talking about today, the emphasis—well, the whole quality—comes from this beautiful shifting of major and minor.

THE TRIAD AS AN EVENT

We're going to do a little work with this wonderful triad. And remember: never, never— I implore you!—forget that a triad is as much of an event as a tone. You've got three tones, you have three events. You have three tones, each with its possibilities of direction. You have three tones quivering *[playing a C-minor triad]* . . . with life. What is going to happen? *[repeating the triad]*. . . . This can happen:

EXAMPLE 18-5. Beethoven, *Piano Sonata in C Minor,* op. 13, "Pathétique," first measure.

. . . . This can happen:

EXAMPLE 18-6. J.S. Bach, *Fugue* from *The Well-Tempered Clavier,* Book 1, no. 2, first two measures.

. . . . This can happen:

EXAMPLE 18-7. J.S. Bach, *Sinfonia* from *Partita in C Minor,* first three beats.

. . . . From this one chord, anything can happen.

You must have this kind of imagination and feeling about the chords you use in working with children, because each one has its emotional impact, each one carries its emotional quality—and we are working with an emotional art. We are working directly on the emotions of children and reaching their spiritual selves, very often through the emotional impact the music has upon them.

FINDING THE RIGHT CHORDS WHEN WRITING MUSIC FOR THERAPY

So, when you write a new good morning song or a goodbye song and harmonize it, think of the great responsibility you have. Never take the easy chord, or the first chord. Take the right chord. You might have to look for it. You might have to play a dozen chords over and over and over until you find just the right one. Composers do this. They are constantly faced with choices.

SINGING NONCHORDAL TONES TO LEAD INTO THE ROMANTIC IDIOM

Now we come to thinking about the kinds of harmonies used in a certain kind of romantic music. I'm not talking about a sentimental music at all. I'm talking about the tenderness romantic music can carry, the tenderness and the warmth, but never sentimentality, never weakness.

Here we must become very sensitive to how we change the harmonies, which will mean changing one of the thirds. A good guide is to move quite quietly, as far as the actual change is concerned, by altering one or possibly two tones.

Combined with this are the nonchordal tones—appoggiaturas, whichever you like—the tones that do not belong to the chord, that you may sing. *[playing a C-minor triad in root position].* . . . Now which tone of the C minor scale is not there . . . ?

Students: A-flat.

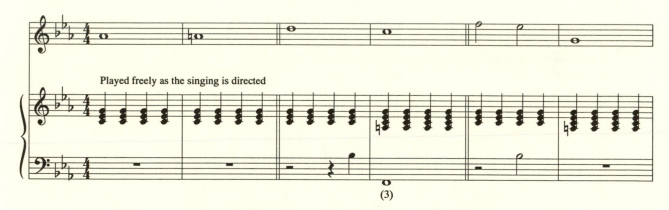

EXAMPLE 18-8. Singing nonchordal tones over a C-minor triad.

. . . . Sing an A♭. . . . *[As the C minor chord is repeated, a student sings A♭ against it.]* . . . Loud, come on . . . good. Everybody do it. *[The class sings the note as the chord is repeated.]* . . . Go up to A♮. . . . *[The class sings A♮ over repetitions of the chord.]* . . . Now we're getting somewhere. Isn't it wonderful!

What other tone can we sing? *[Class members sing a variety of tones softly as the C minor chord is struck again.]* . . . Say it first and then sing it, so I can hear it. Just one person.

Sissel:	D.
Paul:	D?
Sissel:	Yes.
Paul:	D. Sing a lovely D, Sissel. *[She sings D above the root of the sustained chord.]* . . . All right, an octave higher—in tune—everybody. . . . *[The class sings D to the C minor chord; then the bass tone C is lowered to B♭, and then to the F an octave and a fourth below (3), with an F dominant chord resulting.]* . . . Down to C. . . . All right, once more: the D . . . *[The class sings D over the C minor chord; the root descends to B♭.]* . . . C . . .

[The sung D resolves to C as the chord falls to F dominant.] . . . We're getting into the idiom. Do you feel it?

Students: Yes!

Paul: Wonderful!

There's also the possibility of the F *[continuing to repeat the C-minor triad]*. . . . Who can hit that high F? All right, the low one. *[The students begin with the lower F but some take the high F over the C-minor triad.]* . . . E♭. . . . *[The voices descend to E♭ as the B♭ is again added to the C minor chord.]* . . . Again: *[The progression is repeated and the voices fall from F to E♭.]* . . . G . . . *[The voices descend to G against the C minor chord with an added A♮.]* . . . We're getting closer, aren't we? Isn't it beautiful! Isn't it beautiful.

So we use nonchordal tones, we sing them against what we are playing. It's very hard to play them and make the same effect. And after all, don't forget, we are going to be the singing therapists—*[laughter from everyone]*. Isn't it wonderful to know that?

All right. Now *[repeating the C minor chord]*, let's sing a line against this. Let's sing:

EXAMPLE 18-9. Exploring the romantic idiom: singing nonchordal tones, developing the harmony, and adding a cadence.

[Repeating the C minor chord and singing the melodic line to (4)]. . . . All right? *[The class sings over the chord progression; the example is extended to a cadence].* . . . Yes, that's right, that's right. Very wonderful and beautiful to sing.

Who hasn't been at the piano this week? Unni, were you? Yes, you were. Sissel, you weren't.

Let's hear some of these. Play each one three times in about the same tempo as I did it. Just—not all of them, perhaps until here *[indicating (5) on the blackboard]*, all right?

continued on next page

continued from preceding page

EXAMPLE 18-10. An exercise in romantic melodic invention and harmonic progression.

[Sissel plays the exercise slowly, repeating each chord three times and playing into the sixth measure.] . . . All right. Now when Sissel plays it again, we're going to sing *[indicating the melodic line]*, all right? Play each chord twice now, just twice. We're going to begin with the C. *[The progression is repeated, with the chords as half notes, and the melody sung as written, until (5).]* . . . That's it. That's it, that's it, that's it. If this doesn't put the right idiom into your bones! Okay, Sissel, good.

    Someone who can play it this fast? Jane Healey? Can we do the next group of chords, from here, to this one? Play it through first alone. Get it? *[Jane plays the progression from the beginning, repeating each chord three times. She increases tempo and dynamics when urged to do so and ends at (6).]* . . . All right, good. You don't need to use so much tone. I just wanted to point out that the left hand was to be repeated, too. All right? *[addressing the class]* Ready! *[As the progression is repeated under direction, the three repetitions of the chord are changed to two repetitions to follow the rhythm of the melodic line. The exercise is stopped at (6).]* . . . Right. Good, good, good!

Do you feel the tenderness in this, the warmth in it? And the care in it?

Jane H.:   It's actually fantastic to sit here and hear it in a circle.
Paul: Isn't it marvelous to hear it! It's too bad they can't all be out here hearing themselves sing it.
Jane H.:   Gosh!
Paul: Now this E♭ (7) was meant to be played, too, as well as sung. You didn't understand that. All right, now can we take it from here (8) to the end? *[Jane plays the progression to the end, repeating each chord three times, and then plays the initial C minor chord.]* Right. Good.

Now we want to sing some more. There's nothing like singing to these things *[writing to extend the melody]*: F, and let's hold it, hold it, and hold it, and hold it. And then down to the A♭, and hold that. E♭, and down to the F again. Perhaps if you play this chord (6), we can get our D♭. *[As the chord is played, the singers begin. The melody is sung with each accompanying chord repeated twice until (9), where the singers falter.]* . . . Let's do the F's again. That's a very hard interval. *[The progression is recommenced and continues, ending on the initial C.]* . . . Yes. Wasn't very good, I didn't lead you very well through it. But it has a beautiful line.

USING ROMANTIC MUSIC TO REACH ADOLESCENTS

These are just suggestions. You can find other tones to sing to them. You can find other chords. This is simply an example for you all to have, of the kind of harmony that is—to my mind—the tenderest, warmest, sweetest, to bring to an adolescent child who needs comfort; who needs the feeling that the music understands her, the music understands him. Understands his turbulent, confused, mixed-up condition, which you get so desperately in the physically handicapped with normal intelligence. When they enter adolescence, they really suffer, and this kind of music can be so meaningful for them. And in this respect I can recommend to you all, for investigation and further study, the songs of Fauré. I think, perhaps, they are even better than studying a Puccini opera, because it's not quite so diffuse. It's not a piano arrangement of an orchestral score, but you get the harmonies right there in the piano part.

THE CULTURAL AND CLINICAL VALUE OF THE SONG LITERATURE

Just to make a little digression, as part of your cultural growth, which you know I view as so important for you all, because you will never have more to give a child than you have within yourself. To put into yourselves a familiarity, a knowledge, an appreciation of the song literature is one of the greatest things a musician can do. Unfortunately, we've come to an age when very few people now give vocal concerts, and when they do the hall is seldom filled. There seems to be a lack of interest now, which is a very sad thing, and also a very telling fact about the age in which we live.

What do we find in songs? A clue to the composer's inner being. He tells us about himself through the poems he has chosen to put to music. How many of you know the *Dichterliebe* of Schumann? Good! Isn't that lovely. I'm so glad. You should all know them— "The Poet's Love"—some of the most beautiful songs ever written. And *Die Frauenliebe und Leben*. How many of you? Ah, again, "The Love and the Life of a Woman," beautifully done by Schumann. And so absolutely different in their poetry from *Die Schöne Müllerin,* which Schubert chose to put to music. Two completely different personalities.

And if you look—if you come to the present day—what does Ravel choose? He chooses some Greek folk songs to put to music, to arrange. He chooses some poems about Don Quixote. He chooses something—they're called *Cinq Histoires Naturelles*—marvelous songs about a peacock and a cricket, and other creatures. Completely different from Debussy, who was setting the poetry of Verlaine, as was Fauré.

So this tremendous literature is there, a treasure for each one of us—and beautiful for everyone's sightreading, incidentally. When you can sightread and sing the vocal part at the same time—marvelous practice.

ON THE DISCERNING APPRECIATION OF SCHUBERT'S SONGS

Amanda: ·When you think that Schubert wrote six hundred songs, and most people just know the *Schwanengesang, Winterreise,* and the *Schöne Müllerin.* Hundreds of others!

Paul: I know. And that wonderful song, *The Doppelgänger.* Do you know that one? In which he's looking at himself? That's a tremendous poem, and a tremendous song.

But Schubert wrote some awfully bad ones, too. I had a wonderful experience in Bavaria when I was twenty-one. One afternoon, in this fabulous house I stayed in, there was a young prince, Ludwig of Hesse. He was studying art in Munich at the university and he'd come down for the weekend. I was reading through some Schubert lieder, alone in the music room, and he came in and he sat down. I saw he was there. And I finished one and I turned to him and said, "That's a bad one, isn't it!" And he turned absolutely white. He held up his hand and said, "Yes, it is, but we were raised to think that every song of Schubert was a great song." And I remember saying, "Isn't it wonderful to find out he was human like the rest of us? He wrote some bad ones, too." Isn't that extraordinary? I shall never forget him. He said, "That's the difference between a German and an American. We're brought up in this tradition, you know, to believe that everything written by a German composer is absolute perfection. But you in America, you're free. You see the bad and choose. You see the good, and you can say it."

Now let's do this once more *[Example 18-10].* Play our first lovely chord, from which anything can happen. *[The initial C minor chord is struck.]* Ready? *[The exercise is played through, ending on the C minor chord.]* Beautiful. Thank you, Jane. Very well done.

AN EXPERIENCE OF THE ROMANTIC IDIOM IN A FAURÉ SONG

I think it speaks for itself. We've all had enough experience with children, and with ourselves. I'm not so old that I can't remember being eighteen. I knew what the songs of Fauré meant to me when I first discovered them. Do you know the *Après un Rêve* of Fauré?

Class: Yes.

Paul: How many of you know it? A few don't. I can't sing it, but I'll do what I can with it. And you will see that I chose deliberately this key *[in Example 18-8],* because it's written in this key. Maybe I should whistle it.

The words are simply: "After a dream"—he dreamt—he had a mirage of happiness in a dream, and he says—"your eyes were sweeter, your voice was pure and sonorous, and you gleamed like the heavens clearing for dawn. You called me, and I left the earth to fly with you into the light. The heavens half-opened for us and showed glimpses of their divinity, but alas, alas—" Of course, he awakes, and he wishes the dream to come back with its lies: "Return, return, mysterious night."

continued on next page

continued from preceding page

EXAMPLE 18-11. Fauré, *Après un Rêve.*

[The song is played and sung in its entirety.] . . . Now that's a beautiful example of romanticism: that wonderful line from the very opening C-minor triad. And you will find beautiful examples all through. There are four volumes of these.

IN CONCLUSION

Well, this is as far as we can go with the idioms in the time we have left, but on the last page of your Part Five *[in Creative Music Therapy]* you will find some suggestions of material to look into. I think you've got a good armory, now, to delve into and work on with the children you will be working with in the future. It's been very exciting for me to have to put these things in a teachable form, the things I did instinctively and musically. It's nice to know that it can be done, can be transmitted, and you in turn can learn to do it. It's been a great pleasure to me.

Clive: Can we sing *Goodbye!* to that last *[harmonic style]*?
Paul: Not very well.

EXAMPLE 18-12. Nordoff and Robbins, *Goodbye!* with romantic developments. Adapted from P. Nordoff and C. Robbins, *The First Book of Children's Play-Songs* (Bryn Mawr, Pa.: Theodore Presser Co., 1962), p. 21.

Paul: Thank you.
Students: Beautiful.

REFERENCES

Nordoff, Paul, & Robbins, Clive (1977). *Creative Music Therapy.* New York: John Day. [Revised and expanded edition in press, St. Louis, Mo.: MMB Music, Inc., 1999.]

Nordoff, Paul, & Robbins, Clive (1983). *Music Therapy in Special Education.* St. Louis, Mo.: MMB Music, Inc.

Nordoff, Paul, & Robbins, Clive (1992). *Therapy in Music for Handicapped Children.* London: Victor Gollancz.

Steiner, Rudolf (1977). Lecture Two in *Eurythmy as Visible Music,* 2nd ed. London: Rudolf Steiner Press.

Yasser, Joseph (1932). Chapters 6 to 8 in *A Theory of Evolving Tonality.* New York: American Library of Musicology.

Zuckerkandl, Victor (1973). *Sound and Symbol: Music and the External World* (W. D. Trask, Trans.). Princeton, N.J.: Princeton University Press.

ADDITIONAL READINGS ON NORDOFF-ROBBINS MUSIC THERAPY

Aigen, Kenneth (1995). The aesthetic foundation of clinical theory. In Carolyn B. Kenny (Ed.), *Listening, Playing, Creating: Essays on the Power of Sound* (pp. 233–257). Albany, N.Y.: State University of New York Press.

Aigen, Kenneth (1995). Cognitive and affective processes activated in music therapy: A preliminary model for contemporary Nordoff-Robbins practice. *Music Therapy, 12,* 16–39.

Aigen, Kenneth (1996). *Being in music: Foundations of Nordoff-Robbins music therapy.* Nordoff-Robbins Music Therapy Monograph Series 1. St. Louis, Mo.: MMB Music, Inc.

Aigen, Kenneth (1997). *Here we are in music: One year with an adolescent, creative music therapy group.* Nordoff-Robbins Music Therapy Monograph Series 2. St. Louis, Mo.: MMB Music, Inc.

Aigen, Kenneth (1998). *Paths of development in Nordoff-Robbins Music Therapy.* Gilsum, N.H.: Barcelona Publishers.

Ansdell, Gary (1995). *Music for life: Aspects of creative music therapy with adult clients.* London, & Bristol, Pa.: Jessica Kingsley Publishers.

Forinash, Michele (1992). A phenomenological analysis of the Nordoff-Robbins approach to music therapy: The lived experience of clinical improvisation. *Music Therapy, 11,* 120–141.

Lee, Colin (1996). *Music at the edge: The music therapy experiences of a musician with AIDS.* London & New York: Routledge.

Nordoff, Paul, & Robbins, Clive (1992). *Therapy in music for handicapped children.* London: Gollancz.

Nordoff, Paul, & Robbins, Clive (1977). *Creative music therapy.* New York: John Day & Co. [This work is out of print but can be purchased through the Nordoff-Robbins Center for Music Therapy at New York University. A second edition, revised, is being published by MMB Music, Inc., in St. Louis, Mo.]

Nordoff, Paul, & Robbins, Clive (1983). *Music therapy in special education.* St. Louis, Mo.: MMB Music, Inc.

Pavlicevic, Mercedes (1997). *Music Therapy in Context: Music, Meaning and Relationship.* London, & Bristol, Pa.: Jessica Kingsley Publishers.

Robbins, Carol, & Robbins, Clive (1991). Creative music therapy in bringing order, change and communicativeness to the life of a brain-injured adolescent. In Kenneth E. Bruscia (Ed.), *Case Studies in Music Therapy* (pp. 231–249). Phoenixville, Pa.: Barcelona Publishers.

Robbins, Carol, & Robbins, Clive (1991). Self-communications in creative music therapy. In Kenneth E. Bruscia (Ed.), *Case Studies in Music Therapy* (pp. 55–72). Phoenixville, Pa.: Barcelona Publishers.

Robbins, Clive (1993). The creative processes are universal. In Margaret Heal & Tony Wigram (Eds.), *Music Therapy in Health and Education* (pp. 7–25). London, & Bristol, Pa.: Jessica Kingsley Publishers.

Robbins, Clive, & Forinash, Michele (1991). A time paradigm: Time as a multilevel phenomenon in music therapy. *Music Therapy, 10,* 46–57.

Robbins, Clive, & Robbins, Carol (1980). *Music for the hearing impaired and other special groups*. St. Louis, Mo.: MMB Music, Inc.

Turry, Alan (1998). Transference and countertransference in Nordoff-Robbins music therapy. In Kenneth E. Bruscia (Ed.), *The Dynamics of Music Psychotherapy* (pp. 161–212). Gilsum, N.H.: Barcelona Publishers.

Turry, Alan, & Ritholz, Michele (1994). The journey by train: Creative music therapy with a 17-year-old boy. *Music Therapy, 12* (2), 58–87.

VIDEOTAPE STUDIES

Aigen, Kenneth. *Improvised Song in Group Music Therapy*. Available through the Nordoff-Robbins Center for Music Therapy at New York University.

CREDITS FOR COPYRIGHTED MATERIAL

Nin-Culmell, Joaquin. Excerpt from *Ball pla i L'esquerrana* from *Tonadas,* Vol. 4, no. 42. Reproduced by permission of the copyright holders, Broude Brothers Limited and Broude International Edition.

Nin-Culmell, Joaquin. Excerpt from *Canción de Labrador* from *Tonadas,* Vol. 1, no. 3. Reproduced by permission of the copyright holders, Broude Brothers Limited and Broude International Edition.

Nin-Culmell, Joaquin. Excerpt from *Copla Asturiana* from *Tonadas,* Vol. 3, no. 26. Reproduced by permission of the copyright holders, Broude Brothers Limited and Broude International Edition.

Nin-Culmell, Joaquin. Excerpt from *Motivo de Santo Domingo* from *Tonadas,* Vol. 3, no. 30. Reproduced by permission of the copyright holders, Broude Brothers Limited and Broude International Edition.

Nin-Culmell, Joaquin. Excerpt from *Pandeirada* from *Tonadas,* Vol. 3, no. 29. Reproduced by permission of the copyright holders, Broude Brothers Limited and Broude International Edition.

Nordoff, Paul. *Thank You.* From P. Nordoff and C. Robbins, *The Third Book of Children's Play-Songs.* (Bryn Mawr, Pa.: Theodore Presser Co., 1980), p. 23. Used with permission.

Nordoff, Paul, and Robbins, Clive. *Goodbye!* From P. Nordoff and C. Robbins, *The First Book of Children's Play-Songs* (Bryn Mawr, Pa.: Theodore Presser Co., 1962), p. 21. Used with permission.

Nordoff, Paul, and Robbins, Clive. *Sweeping Song.* From "Pif-Paf-Poltrie" (Bryn Mawr, Pa.: Theodore Presser Co., 1969). Used with permission.

Ravel, Maurice. Excerpts from *Alborado del Grazioso* from *Miroirs.* © 1905 Editions Max Eschig. Used By Permission. Sole Agent, U.S.A., Theodore Presser Company.

Ravel, Maurice. Excerpt from *Chanson Epique* from *Don Quichotte à Dulcinée.* © 1933 Durand S.A. Editions Musicales. Editions A.R.I.M.A. & Durand S.A. Editions Musicales. Joint Publication. Used By Permission. Sole Agent U.S.A., Theodore Presser Company.

Ravel, Maurice. Excerpts from *Menuet* from *Sonatine.* © 1905 Editions Max Eschig. Used By Permission. Sole Agent, U.S.A., Theodore Presser Company.

Ravel, Maurice. Excerpts from *Pavanne of the Sleeping Beauty.* © 1910 Durand S.A. Editions Musicales. Editions A.R.I.M.A. & Durand S.A. Editions Musicales. Joint Publication. Used By Permission. Sole Agent U.S.A., Theodore Presser Company.

Stern, James (Ed.), *The Complete Grimm's Fairy Tales* (Margaret Hunt, Trans.). New York: Random House, 1972. The story of "Fair Katrinelje and Pif-Paf-Poltrie" described on p. 110 is paraphrased from this source.

Yasser, Joseph. *A Theory of Evolving Tonality* (New York: American Library of Musicology, 1932), Chapters 6 to 8. The majority of references in Explorations Fourteen and Fifteen relating to the pentatonic, its place in the historical development of music, and its harmonization are drawn from this source.